CHAD
in Pictures

Christine Zuchora-Walske

Twenty-First Century Books

Contents

Website address: www.lernerbooks.co

Twenty-First Century Books
A division of Lerner Publishing Group, Inc.
241 First Avenue North
Minneapolis, MN 55401 U.S.A.

web enhanced @ www.vgsbooks.com

CULTURAL LIFE 48

▶ Religion. Language. Literature. Music and Dance. Food. Art and Architecture. Sports and Recreation. Holidays and Festivals.

THE ECONOMY 58

▶ Industry. Services. Agriculture. Foreign Trade. Transportation. Communications. The Future.

FOR MORE INFORMATION

Library of Congress Cataloging-in-Publication Data

Zuchora-Walske, Christine.
    Chad in pictures / by Christine Zuchora-Walske.
      p. cm. – (Visual geography series)
    Includes bibliographical references and index.
  ISBN 978-1-57505-956-3 (lib. bdg. : alk. paper)
    1. Chad—Juvenile literature. 2. Chad—Geography—Juvenile literature. 3. Chad—History—Juvenile literature. 4. Chad—Pictorial works—Juvenile literature. I. Title.
  DT546.422.Z83 2009
  967.43—dc22   2008031014

4768

Manufactured in the United States of America
1 2 3 4 5 6 – BP – 14 13 12 11 10 09

INTRODUCTION

Chad, a large nation in north central Africa, is a land of stunning variety and stark beauty. Within its borders lie tropical forests, swampy river valleys, broad grasslands, long lakeshores, sandy deserts, and rugged mountains. Elephants, ostriches, and lions roam the nation's plains and woods. Crocodiles and hippos live in its waters.

Chad's human landscape is as rich as its natural landscape. The culture of Chad reflects its long history of human habitation. For tens of thousands of years, this land at the crossroads of Africa has welcomed millions of migrants. It has given birth to countless societies. Some peoples were wandering hunters, gatherers, and herders. Others were settled farmers and fishers. Still others were fearsome warriors or slave traders.

For thousands of years, new people moved into Chad from the north and east. As migrants mingled with the local people, they formed new bloodlines, languages, and cultures. Eventually, more than one hundred distinct ethnic groups emerged. Empires rose and fell, often battling one another for control.

web enhanced @ www.vgsbooks.com

In the late 1800s, a new wave of people arrived—this time from distant Europe. The French sought land, natural resources, and workers they could use to enrich their own empire. By then all Chad's major kingdoms were in decline. They resisted French forces for several years. But one by one, they finally submitted in defeat. From 1900 to 1960, Chad endured colonial rule by France.

The French had little respect for Chad's existing societies. The French drew new borders, carving up historic realms and dividing ethnic groups. French officials exploited the native people, often resettling entire villages and forcing Chadians to labor on public works. The French replaced local chiefs and councils with French or French-appointed officials. For decades these officials made laws and decisions that favored France and its colonists over Chad and its native people.

Chad's time as a French colony was short compared to its long history. But this period left a permanent mark on the nation. France did little to build economic, political, or cultural cooperation in its colony.

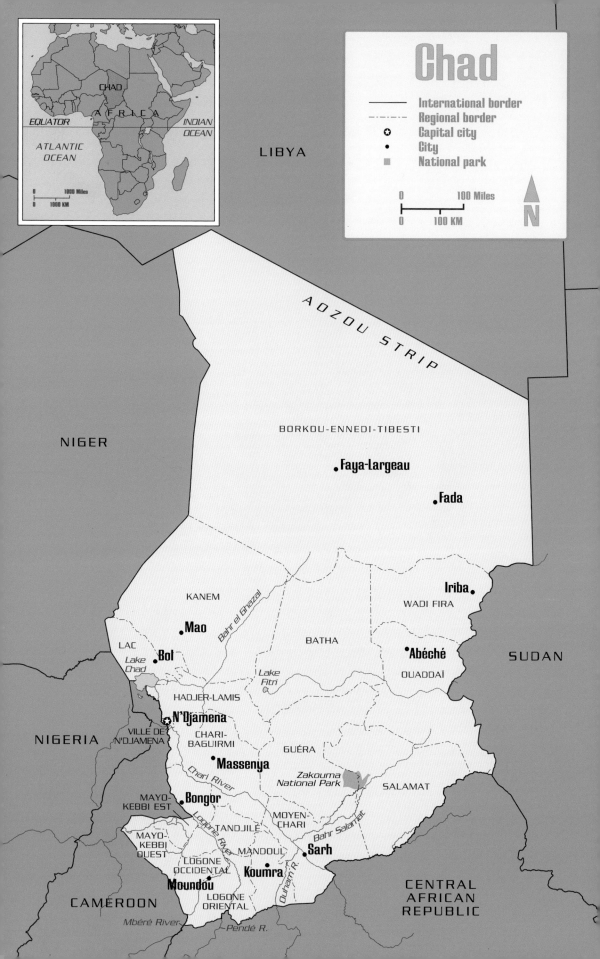

When independence came in 1960, Chadians inherited a huge territory that had scarce resources, a poor population, widespread ethnic tensions, and few public services. The people of Chad needed leaders who could unify them and help them improve their lives. Instead, their leaders ushered in decades of civil war, political unrest, and limited freedom.

Chad's ongoing conflicts—not only among Chadian ethnic groups but also between Chad and its neighbors—have left it one of the world's poorest nations. Hunger is common, health and education are dismal, and life expectancy is short. An exploding population—almost 11 million and growing quickly—complicates the nation's challenges. To make matters worse, 5 percent of people in Chad have fled wars there and in neighboring countries. They depend on aid for survival.

Amid this turmoil, the government struggles to develop a fledgling oil industry in hopes of boosting Chad's entire economy. Chadians hope their leaders will manage this resource wisely, using it to improve living conditions for everyone. Success at this task will pave the way for political healing and lasting peace and freedom.

THE LAND

The name *Chad*, which means "lake" in a local language, reveals much about Chad's land. Chad, Africa's fifth-largest nation, lies in north central Africa. The country sits almost entirely within the Lake Chad Basin, a hollow that once contained a large sea. Niger, Nigeria, and Cameroon form Chad's western border. The Central African Republic lies to the south, Sudan to the east, and Libya to the north.

Chad is landlocked, with no outlet to the ocean. Its borders are distant from all the seas that surround Africa. The capital city, N'Djamena, is 684 miles (1,100 kilometers) from the Atlantic Ocean. Abéché, a city in eastern Chad, lies 1,647 miles (2,650 km) from the Red Sea. Fay-Largeau in northern Chad sits in the middle of the Sahara, 963 miles (1,550 km) from the Mediterranean Sea.

Chad stretches 1,087 miles (1,750 km) from north to south and 777 miles (1,250 km) from east to west. The country covers an area of 495,755 square miles (1,284,000 sq. km). It's about the same size as the states of Washington, Oregon, Idaho, Montana, and Wyoming combined.

◉ Topography

Chad is a land of great variety. It has mountains, desert, and a high, flat plateau. The Lake Chad Basin is the nation's dominant topographical feature. This vast hollow extends in all directions from Lake Chad, on Chad's western border. The basin forms a low, sandy plain that covers most of Chad. Within the basin, elevations range from 525 feet (160 meters) above sea level to 1,640 feet (500 m).

Along Chad's northern, eastern, and southern borders, an arc of highlands encloses the Lake Chad Basin. The Tibesti Mountains rise in northwestern Chad. They form the largest and highest mountain range in the Sahara, a large desert that covers much of northern Africa. The highest peak in this range and in Chad is Emi Koussi at 11,204 feet (3,415 m). The Tibesti Mountains are dormant (inactive) volcanoes. They're famous for their weathered black rock, as well as for their geysers (fountains of steam and hot water that shoot into the air) and hot springs.

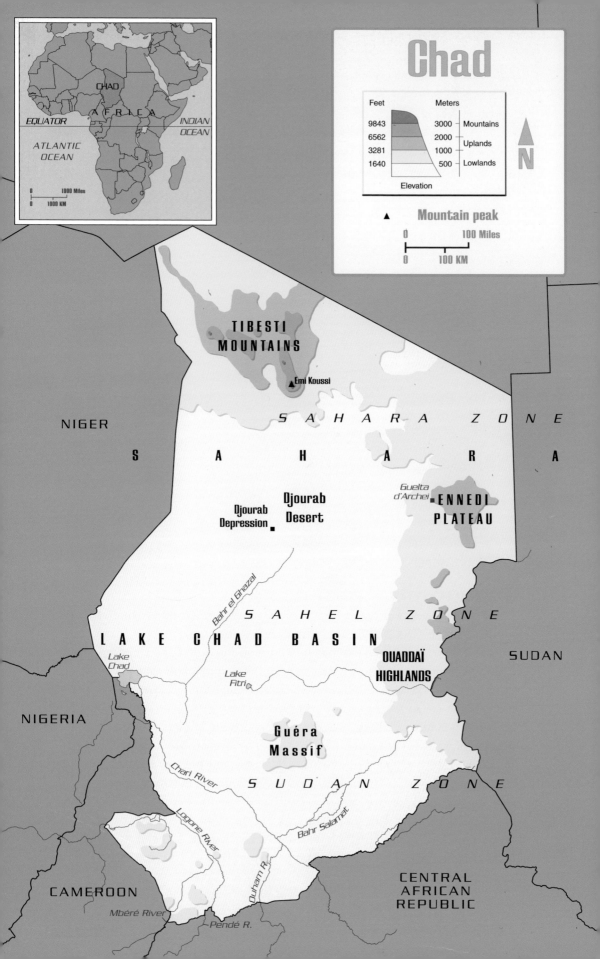

This volcano is part of the Tibesti Mountains.

The southern boundary of the Lake Chad Basin lies just outside Chad's southern border. Inside the border, the isolated Guéra Massif rises to 5,292 feet (1,613 m). It towers over the surrounding lowlands.

The Ennedi Plateau marks Chad's northeastern corner. A plateau is an elevated plain. This sandstone tableland rises from the Lake Chad Basin in a series of steps. The region climbs to 4,756 feet (1,450 m) and includes hundreds of natural arches and other rock formations. Wind, rain, flowing water, and blowing sand carved these sculptures over thousands of years.

Aloba Arch, a sandstone formation on the Ennedi Plateau, is one of the biggest natural arches in the world. It's about 250 feet (76 m) long and almost 400 feet (122 m) tall.

The Ouaddaï Highlands stretch along Chad's eastern border. They separate the watersheds (drained areas) of the Nile River and the rivers that flow into Lake Chad. This region contains windswept plateaus and peaks up to 4,331 feet (1,320 m). Like the Ennedi Plateau, the Ouaddaï Highlands include many fantastic rock formations.

The arc of highlands ends in Chad's southwestern corner. There the foothills of the Adamawa and Mandara mountains rise along the Cameroon border.

◉ Rivers and Lakes

Chad's rivers form two main systems: the Chari and Logone. Both river systems flow from the southeast into Lake Chad.

The Chari River is about 750 miles (1,207 km) long. It begins with several headstreams in the Central African Republic. These streams join near Chad's southern border. As the Chari continues flowing northwestward, the Ouham River and the Bahr Salamat join it. Near Chad's western border with Cameroon, the Chari enters a large swamp. When it reaches the city of N'Djamena, it joins the Logone River.

The Logone River is about 600 miles (966 km) long. It forms in Chad at the junction of the Pendé River, which begins in the Central African Republic, and the Mbéré River, which begins in Cameroon. The Logone flows mainly through swampland along the Chad-Cameroon border until it joins the Chari River at N'Djamena. As the Chari-Logone River approaches Lake Chad, it splits into several branches to form a wide delta (land formed by sediment deposited by a river).

Lake Chad lies roughly in the middle of Chad's western border. About ten thousand years ago, it filled much of the Lake Chad Basin. It has shrunk and expanded many times with changing climate conditions. Since the mid-1900s, it has shrunk dramatically. In 1963 it covered the borderland where Chad, Niger, Nigeria, and Cameroon meet. Since then it has shrunk 90 percent and lies only within Chad. Drought (lack of rain) and human demand for drinking and irrigation

The Chari River flows northwestward to N'Djamena and eventually into Lake Chad.

A boy drinks from **Lake Chad.** Lake Chad is the primary source of water for a large part of western Chad, as well as for neighboring countries.

water are responsible for this shrinkage. Lake Chad's current area hovers around 772 square miles (2,000 sq. km). Its much smaller neighbor, Lake Fitri, is suffering from the same fate.

Central and northern Chad contain no other permanent rivers or large natural lakes. These regions do, however, have many wadis (seasonal streams) and small lakes fed by springs and occasional rain. These parts of Chad are also home to *gueltas*. A guelta, or desert wetland, forms when lowlands meet an underground water source, creating a permanent pool.

Climate

Two large air masses interact over Africa to create Chad's climate. A mass of moist air forms over the Atlantic Ocean west of the continent. A mass of dry air forms over

SAND DAM

Surprisingly, Lake Chad does not lie in the lowest part of the Lake Chad Basin. The lake's surface is about 925 feet (282 m) above sea level. The lowest part of the basin, the Djourab Depression, northeast of the lake, is 400 feet (122 m) lower. Lake Chad doesn't flow into it because an *erg* (sea of sand dunes) creates a dam between the lake and the hollow.

Africa. A front (boundary) forms where the masses meet. Rain tends to fall along this front.

A seasonal wind reversal called the West African Monsoon pushes the front to different positions throughout the year. From November to March, a dry northeasterly wind blows off Africa toward the Atlantic. This wind pushes the front offshore, causing a dry season in northern and western Africa. From April to October, a moist southwesterly wind blows off the Atlantic toward Africa. This wind pushes the front inland, causing a rainy season.

In July the front may travel as far inland as central Chad, bringing rain to the southern two-thirds of the country. From November to March, the front exits Chad, taking the rain with it. This pattern creates three distinct climate zones. They are the Sudan zone in the south, the Sahel zone in central Chad, and the Sahara zone in the north.

The Sudan zone covers the southern third of Chad. Its rainy season lasts from April to October. This zone gets annual rainfall of 24 to 49 inches (60 to 125 centimeters). Temperatures range from 57°F to 102°F (14° to 39°C). The Sahel zone covers the central third of Chad. Its rainy season lasts from June to September. This zone gets annual rainfall of 8 to 35 inches (20 to 90 cm). Though the Sahel gets less rain, its temperature range is the same as the Sudan zone's.

November brings the harmattan to Chad. This dry, hot wind blows southward from the Sahara. It carries with it fine sand and dust, sometimes resulting in a thin haze that covers the land.

The Sahara zone covers the northern third of Chad. It has no rainy season. Rain comes via occasional storms unrelated to the monsoon. This zone gets annual rainfall of 0.4 to 8 inches (1 to 20 cm). Rainfall tends to be greater at higher elevations, and snow is fairly common on the highest peaks. Temperatures generally range from 41°F to 99°F (5° to 37°C), but the Sahara is prone to extremes. It can get as hot as 122°F (50°C) and as cold as 14°F (–10°C). Within twenty-four hours, daytime and nighttime temperatures can differ up to 68°F (38°C).

Flora and Fauna

Because Chad's climate varies from tropical (warm and wet) in the south to desert in the north, the nation is home to a wide array of plants and animals. About 1,600 different plant species (kinds) and 772 animal species live there. Chad's animals include about 134 kinds of mammals, 141 bird species, 52 kinds of reptiles, 30 amphibian species, and 130 kinds of fish. The flora and fauna in any region of Chad reflect the amount of rain the area gets.

The warm, wet climate of the Sudan zone supports a patchwork of savanna (grassland), forest, and swamp. Trees in the far south are mostly broadleafs such as African birch trees. Thornbushes such as acacia are more common in the northern part of the zone. Farming has taken over much of this region. Sorghum and millet are common grain crops here. Many farmers also grow legumes (beans and peas), sesame, and vegetables.

The **African wildcat lives throughout Africa's Sahara and Sahel, including in Chad. Scientists believe this small cat is the ancestor of the modern domestic cat.**

The forests and savannas of the Sudan zone shelter many large animals. These include antelopes, elephants, giraffes, Cape buffalo, rhinoceroses, and lions. Millions of birds—from sparrows to ostriches to cranes—nest in and migrate through this region. Its rivers, lakes, and swamps teem with fish and frogs. Hippopotamuses, Nile crocodiles, and freshwater manatees (large aquatic mammals distantly related to elephants) live there too.

A herd of elephants travels through Zakouma National Park in southern Chad.

The drier climate of the Sahel zone supports mostly shortgrass savanna. Grasses and large thornbushes dominate the southern Sahel. Some farmers grow sorghum and millet here. The northern Sahel supports grasses, herbs, and low shrubs. Farmers raise date palms, grains, fruits, and vegetables in scattered oases (small, green areas surrounding natural springs).

Many smaller animals live in central Chad's grasslands. Rodents thrive there. Antelopes, foxes, jackals, hyenas, and African wildcats are common. So are birds such as bee-eaters and bustards. Lake Chad hosts waterfowl, fish, otters, hippos, and crocodiles. A few elephants, giraffes, lions, and leopards graze and hunt along the shores. Farmers and herders in the Sahel raise cattle, sheep, goats, and chickens.

The desert climate of the Sahara zone supports only sparse grasses and herbs. Scattered oases and wells nourish groves of date palms and fruit trees as well as small plots of grain and vegetables. Northern Chad's wild animals include antelopes, wild asses, and Barbary sheep. Camels and cattle are common domestic animals.

Groves of **date palms** grow in the Sahara around oases. This oasis supports the city of Faya-Largeau.

Natural Resources

Throughout the centuries, Chad's key natural resources have been its land and waters. Chad has always had a mostly rural society. Its people rely heavily on farming and fishing for their survival. Farmers grow crops on about half the country's land. They raise livestock on the rest. Chad's shrinking rivers and lakes still provide water, food, and income for many thousands of people.

Chad's energy resources are lopsided. The nation is rich in oil and is one of Africa's top oil producers (although war and instability prevented Chad from extracting this resource until 2003). But the nation has no hydroelectricity (water-powered energy) and no coal or natural gas deposits. Chad has barely tapped its great solar power potential. Most Chadians supply their energy needs by burning animal dung or wood—both limited resources.

Strife has also prevented Chad from developing its wealth of mineral resources. Companies actively mine for nonmetal minerals—such as natron (a salt used in ceramics and detergents), kaolin (a white clay), limestone, salt, sand, stone, and gravel. But the country has only begun to tap its stores of uranium (a radioactive metal), gold, tungsten (used in electronics), tin, bauxite (aluminum ore), silver, iron ore, and titanium (a very strong, lightweight metal).

KURI CATTLE

Along the shores of Lake Chad, farmers raise Kuri cattle for milk and meat. These cattle have huge, bulbous, hollow horns. The horns can grow as long as 51 inches (130 cm) and as wide as 22 inches (55 cm). Over many centuries, farmers have bred Kuri cattle to encourage this trait. These animals spend their days swimming from island to island in search of food. Their hollow horns help them float.

Environmental Issues

Chad faces serious environmental challenges, including the drying up of Lake Chad. Many of these problems are a result of widespread poverty and high population growth.

An ever-growing number of poor Chadians require food, shelter, and other needs just to survive. To supply their needs, people cut down trees. This not only opens up farmland and pasture but also provides fuel and building material. Some people plow the savanna to grow crops. Many Chadians irrigate their fields by drawing water from the country's lakes and rivers.

Heavy deforestation (clearing of forest), farming, and irrigation contribute to desertification, or drylands turning to barren desert. Chad's Sahel zone is steadily changing from savanna to desert. Native plants are vanishing. Soil is quickly eroding (washing or blowing away). Salt is building up in the soil and water. Underground water sources are dwindling, and lakes are drying up. Since the 1970s, unpredictable rainfall and drought have made these problems worse. About 60 percent of Chad's Sahel zone has become desert. Another 30 percent is vulnerable to desertification.

As suitable habitat dwindles, so does wildlife. Chad was once home to great herds and flocks of animals. But its elephants, lions, cheetahs, hippos, and more are vanishing. Twenty-four of Chad's native animal species are currently threatened. The addax and the dama gazelle (both antelope species), as well as the black rhino, are critically endangered, which means they may die out. Another antelope, the scimitar-horned oryx, is already extinct in the wild. It survives only in captivity. Poaching (illegal hunting) worsens the problem of dwindling wildlife.

To help preserve its wildlife, Chad's government has created four national parks, nine wildlife reserves, twelve protected forests and wetlands, and thirteen reforestation areas. The best known of these areas is Zakouma National Park in southern Chad.

Visit www.vgsbooks.com for links to websites with more information on the environmental challenges facing Chad. See pictures of native Chadian animals that are in danger of vanishing.

Cities

N'DJAMENA (population 759,993) is Chad's capital and its largest city. It lies at the junction of the Chari and Logone rivers, near the town of Kousséri, Cameroon. N'Djamena is about 62 miles (100 km) south of Lake Chad.

People have lived along the Chari River for thousands of years. However, the settlement that became N'Djamena is fairly new. French military commander Émile Gentil founded it in 1900 after France won control of Chad. Gentil named the town Fort-Lamy after his fellow officer Amédée-François Lamy, who died in the Battle of Kousséri. In 1973, several years after Chad gained independence from France, Chadians renamed the city after the Arabic name of a nearby village. (Arabic is a language that originated on the Arabian Peninsula and that is spoken over a large geographic area.) Several destructive battles in Chad's recurring civil war have taken place in N'Djamena.

N'Djamena is the center of Chad's administrative, cultural, and business activities. It houses the national government offices, two universities, and the National Museum. It's a commercial and agricultural hub.

Its main industry is meat processing, and it also serves as a regional market for livestock, salt, dates, and grain. N'Djamena is the center of Chad's transportation system as well. Two transcontinental highways under construction intersect here. N'Djamena International Airport lies on the city's outskirts.

MOUNDOU (population 142,462), Chad's second-largest city, is also the capital of Logone Occidental region (a division similar to a state) in the southwest. It lies on the Logone River, about 300 miles (483 km) south of N'Djamena. Located in Chad's cotton farming belt, the city has developed as an industrial center. In 1939 the French established a cotton research institute here. Moundou is home to Cotontchad, a large state-owned company that processes cotton and manufactures cottonseed soap and oil. The successful Gala Brewery (established in 1964), a cigarette company, and a farm equipment factory are also here. Moundou has an airport with a paved runway. It lies on a main road that connects it with several cities in Chad and Cameroon. The Logone River links Moundou with N'Djamena.

SARH (population 108,061) is the nation's third-largest city. It's the capital of Moyen-Chari region in south central Chad. It lies on the Chari River about 350 miles (563 km) southeast of N'Djamena. The city began about 1930 as Fort-Archambault, a settlement for Chadians returning from forced labor on the Congo-Ocean Railway to the south. The modern name Sarh honors the city's dominant ethnic group, the Sara. The city is home to a museum and several educational institutions. Its economy relies on cloth making, fishing, and livestock trading. Sarh is also a transport hub. It has an airport, and it lies on the main highway from N'Djamena to Bangui, capital of the Central African Republic.

ABÉCHÉ (population 78,191), Chad's fourth-largest city, is the capital of the Ouaddaï region in the east. It lies about 75 miles (120 km) from the border with the country of Sudan. Abéché has a long history. It was the capital of a small kingdom in the 1500s. In the 1600s, it became part of the powerful Ouaddaï Kingdom—and eventually the capital in the 1890s. During this period, it was a hub for the Arab slave trade. A caravan route across the Sahara linked it with the Mediterranean Sea. Historic buildings and ruins still exist in Abéché alongside its modern structures. These include a meatpacking plant, a hospital, a university, a museum, many schools and places of worship, and an airport. Abéché is the headquarters for delivering aid to hundreds of thousands of war refugees living in camps along the Sudanese border.

HISTORY AND GOVERNMENT

Archaeologists found the world's oldest known hominid (humanlike) fossil in Chad. This skull, unearthed from the Djourab Desert in western Chad, is about seven million years old. Other sites in this desert have produced hominid fossils that are at least three million years old.

About ten thousand years ago, Chad was part of an area of Asia and Africa where many early humans settled. Chad's climate was much wetter then. Lake Chad was much bigger too. People lived all along its shores, hunting and farming as well as making tools, pottery, and rock paintings. Ancient rock art in modern northern Chad shows that these people shared their land with elephants, rhinoceroses, giraffes, cattle, and camels.

◉ Sao Civilization

About 2000 B.C., the climate of the Lake Chad Basin was growing drier and the lake was shrinking. Slave raiders from the north began terrorizing the basin's residents. In search of better pastures and refuge from

slavers, the nomadic (wandering) cattle herders of the northern basin began moving south.

Herders began settling in the southern basin in about 1500 B.C. They also began farming. By 1000 B.C., these people had spread south of Lake Chad, and by 500 B.C., their settlements had become towns. The towns were short-lived. Lifestyles shifted back and forth between nomadic and settled. Five hundred years later, permanent towns emerged.

By A.D. 500, the towns south of Lake Chad formed the Sao civilization (highly developed society). This was the earliest known civilization in Chad. Sao communities were small, loosely linked chiefdoms. The people saw their chiefs as divine (holy or godlike) rulers.

The Sao were skilled builders, potters, and metalworkers. They built large clay buildings and thick clay walls to protect their towns. They made clay statues of humans and animals, decorative household ceramics, and huge clay storage and burial pots (similar to coffins).

Their iron, bronze, and copper work included sculptures, coins, household tools, jewelry, and spears.

Sao civilization thrived from the 600s through the 800s. During this time, Arab nomads from the north and east began to settle in the region. As the groups intermarried, the Sao faded as a separate society. The people and their culture blended into the new kingdoms taking shape.

The Rise of Empires

Around 800, Chad's scattered chiefdoms began merging into larger kingdoms. These kingdoms relied on strong armies—especially cavalry (mounted soldiers)—for survival. Most of them, like the Sao, had rulers whom the people considered divine.

The various kingdoms covered northern and central Chad. Their economies depended on controlling the trade routes that crossed the Sahara, linking central Africa with the Mediterranean Sea. None of the kingdoms reached far into southern Chad. In the south, thick forests and disease-spreading insects made it hard for cavalry to operate.

Many empires (large kingdoms) rose and fell after 800. The strongest and longest lasting of these were the Kanem-Bornu Empire, the Baguirmi Kingdom, and the Ouaddaï Kingdom.

The Kanem Empire

The Kanem Empire began when chiefdoms on Lake Chad's northeastern shore formed an alliance called Kanem. The alliance founded a capital city, N'jimi, near the site of modern Mao.

The ruler of Kanem held the title *mai* (king). Kanem's first known king was Mai Sef. About 800 the kingdom grew powerful under Sef's son, Mai Dugu. Dugu was the first king of the Duguwa dynasty (ruling family).

During the 900s, Arabs were still moving to the Lake Chad Basin from the north and east. These migrants, as well as northern African traders, brought Islam with them. (Islam is a religion founded by the Arab prophet Muhammad in the 600s.)

In the late 1000s, a Kanem nobleman named Hummay became a Muslim (follower of Islam). About 1080 Hummay and his Muslim supporters overthrew the Duguwa king. This act not only began a new dynasty, called the Sayfawa, it also made Kanem a Muslim empire.

Kanem's laws changed to follow Islamic codes. Mai Hummay pressured people to become Muslims. Many resisted, preferring to keep their animist religion. (Animists believe spirits inhabit natural places, beings, things, and the everyday world.) Some nobles and their supporters left the empire and moved eastward.

Despite this rift, the empire grew even stronger. Islam brought fresh ideas to Kanem society and government. During the 1100s, the reenergized kingdom expanded westward and southward. Rulers traveled often throughout the realm to display their power and confirm their subjects' loyalty.

The Kanem Empire peaked in the mid-1200s, during the reign of Mai Dunama Dabbalemi. Dabbalemi was a clever ruler and a mighty warrior. To gain better control of Saharan trade routes, Dabbalemi set out to conquer Kanem's neighbors. By the end of his reign, Kanem stretched northward to Fezzan (in modern Libya), westward to Kano (in modern Nigeria), eastward to the Ouaddaï Highlands, and southward to the Adamawa foothills. All the trade routes in northern Africa had to pass through the expanded empire. Dabbalemi granted his military commanders the right to govern the people they conquered. This strategy promoted success, ensured loyalty, and prevented power struggles among the commanders.

After Dabbalemi's death, quarrels among his sons weakened the Sayfawa dynasty. Their feuding soon spiraled into civil war. Amid this chaos, the Kanem Empire's outer territories broke away.

◉ Kanem-Bornu

By the late 1300s, internal power struggles and external attacks were shredding the Kanem Empire. Invaders from the Bulala Kingdom to the east killed several of Kanem's mais during this period. Many mais within a short time produced many claimants to the throne. As these men and their supporters jockeyed for power, civil war erupted again.

By 1400 the Bulala had forced the Sayfawa dynasty out of N'jimi. Mai Umar ibn Idris moved his people to Bornu, on the western shore of Lake Chad (in modern Niger and Nigeria). He established a new capital there and tried to rebuild his kingdom. The kingdom became known as Kanem-Bornu.

Kanem-Bornu struggled through most of the 1400s. Sixteen mais reigned before Mai Ali Gaji overpowered all his rivals in 1497. Gaji's army defeated the Bulala and regained much of Kanem, including the city of N'jimi. The capital, however, remained at N'gazargamu in Bornu. The land there was more fertile and better for raising cattle.

During the 1500s, the Sayfawa dynasty grew stronger than ever. The Kanem-Bornu Empire peaked during the reign of Mai Idris Aluma from 1571 to 1603. Aluma was a brilliant warrior and diplomat. He introduced several new military tactics, which both expanded and strengthened the empire. He established relations with several Mediterranean kingdoms. This diplomacy promoted peace and encouraged trade.

Aluma was a skilled politician at home. He sought smart and loyal allies. He strengthened alliances by arranging marriages. He made major political figures live at the royal court, where he could monitor them. He assembled an advisory council of clan leaders (the heads of major family groups).

Aluma was also a devoted Muslim. He reformed the kingdom's laws to match his beliefs more closely. He built many mosques, or Muslim houses of worship. He also built lodgings in the city of Cairo, Egypt, to help his subjects make pilgrimages (religious journeys) to Mecca. Mecca is a holy city on the Arabian Peninsula. Islam requires each Muslim to visit Mecca once, if possible.

The Kanem-Bornu Empire grew very strong and rich under Aluma. It earned a great deal of income by taxing or looting its conquered territories. It also earned money by taxing its trade routes and participating in the trade itself. The empire sold slaves, natron, cotton, kola nuts, ivory, ostrich feathers, perfume, wax, and animal hides. It bought salt, horses, silk, glass, guns, and copper. Aluma used his wealth to improve agriculture, transportation, and security throughout the kingdom.

After Aluma's death, the Kanem-Bornu Empire stayed strong for a few decades. Then internal tensions and outside pressures began to weaken it. Over the next two centuries, the empire gradually shrank.

◉ The Baguirmi and Ouaddaï Kingdoms

The Baguirmi Kingdom was one of Aluma's conquered territories. As a tributary state, it paid Kanem-Bornu for military protection. However, Baguirmi remained a separate kingdom with its own ruler and capital. Its ruler held the title *mbang* (king). Its capital city was Massenya. Like Kanem-Bornu, Baguirmi was an Islamic kingdom.

Baguirmi broke free of Kanem-Bornu in the mid-1600s. For about a century, Baguirmi expanded. It overcame small neighboring chiefdoms and allied with nearby nomadic peoples.

Meanwhile, the Ouaddaï Kingdom was taking shape to the northeast, in the Ouaddaï Highlands. It began as a kingdom of animists ruled by the Tunjur dynasty. In 1635 several small Muslim groups joined forces to overthrow this dynasty. Ouaddaï then became an Islamic realm. Its ruler held the title *kolak* (king).

Throughout the 1600s and 1700s, Ouaddaï was a tributary state of its eastern neighbor, Darfur (in modern Sudan). In the late 1700s, Ouaddaï broke free and began expanding quickly.

About 1800, during the reign of Kolak Sabun, a new Saharan trade route developed. This route linked Ouaddaï with Benghazi, a Mediterranean city in modern Libya. By taxing the traders who used this route, Ouaddaï grew rich. Sabun also assembled royal caravans to take part directly in the trading. He exchanged slaves kidnapped from the south for armor, guns, and North African military advisers.

As Ouaddaï grew rich and strong, it threatened its western neighbors, including Baguirmi. Baguirmi was suffering from internal quarrels, and it had once again become a tributary state of Kanem-Bornu. Baguirmi accepted military help from Ouaddaï in exchange for becoming its tributary instead of Kanem-Bornu's.

In 1838 a dispute erupted among claimants to the throne of Ouaddaï. Darfur took advantage of this

THE SLAVE TRADE

Slavery and slave trading have thrived in Chad for more than three thousand years. Evidence shows that the business of human trafficking (buying and selling) began there before the Sao civilization and continues in modern times.

Through much of Chad's history, Arabs from the north kidnapped untold numbers of black Africans from the south. They force-marched captives through the Sahara to trading ports on Africa's Mediterranean coast. Many of these slaves died along the way.

Slavery and its related kidnapping and commerce thrived in Chad from about 1500 to 1900. Though slavery officially ended with French rule, it continued informally. The French had little control over Chad's remote areas, and slave raids continued there. The French themselves forced Chadians to labor on public works.

In the early twenty-first century, child slavery persists underground in Chad. Children sold by their desperately poor families or kidnapped from them end up as household servants, cattle herders, clerks, fishers, or sex workers.

infighting. It backed Muhammad al-Sharif, a claimant whom Darfur believed would do its bidding. This ploy backfired. Kolak Sharif rejected Darfur's meddling and made his own decisions. Sharif earned the respect and loyalty of Ouaddaï this way. He went on to become the kingdom's most skilled ruler.

The Fall of Empires

By the early 1800s, Kanem-Bornu was disintegrating. It had lost control of its eastern territories to the Ouaddaï Kingdom. The Fulani Empire had steadily advanced from the west, eventually conquering Kanem-Bornu's capital at N'gazargamu.

Muhammad al-Kanem, a non-Sayfawa warlord and Muslim scholar, tried to salvage the kingdom. He formed an alliance of several ethnic groups to resist the Fulani. This alliance built a capital at Kuka (modern Kukawa, Nigeria).

Though Kanem really ruled the kingdom, Sayfawa mais remained honorary kings until 1846. In that year, Mai Ali Dalatumi started a civil war with help from Ouaddaï. Kanem's forces triumphed. His son Umar became king, ending the Sayfawa dynasty.

This mid-nineteenth-century illustration by a German explorer shows a chief and his warriors of the Kanem-Bornu Empire.

Umar shied away from the ancient title mai. He preferred the simpler title *shehu* (chief). He became known as Shehu Umar al-Bornu. He was neither as wise nor as energetic as his father, and he gradually gave up power to his viziers (advisers). Under Umar and his sons, government disorder, regional squabbling, and Ouaddaï attacks weakened the kingdom.

In 1879 the Sudanese warlord Rabih Fadlallah fled Darfur, whose rulers wanted him dead. Fadlallah created a kingdom for himself south of Ouaddaï. In the 1880s, he tried—but failed—to conquer Ouaddaï. So his realm grew southward and westward instead.

In 1892 Fadlallah's forces attacked Baguirmi. They destroyed its capital, Massenya, in 1893. Baguirmi's king, Mbang Abd ar-Rahman Gwarang, asked France for protection. France, which controlled some land along Africa's western coast, wanted to expand its empire. France agreed to make Baguirmi a protectorate or defend Baguirmi in return for control of Baguirmi's foreign relations.

Later in 1893, Fadlallah attacked and conquered Kanem-Bornu. His forces looted and destroyed the capital at Kuka. Fadlallah established a new capital for his kingdom in the nearby city of Dikwa. There he built a palace, filled the government with Sudanese officers, and reformed the empire's finances. He also earned a reputation as a brutal dictator, pillager, and slave trader.

The French kept advancing throughout the 1890s, gaining more land and influence in Africa. The defeated people of Kanem-Bornu and Baguirmi did not oppose the French. They viewed France as a counterbalance to both Fadlallah and Ouaddaï. Ouaddaï, for its part, kept resisting Fadlallah and pressing westward. It strongly opposed the French advance.

▶ French Conquest

By the late 1800s, several European nations had colonies (dependent territories) in Africa. They farmed parts of the continent's land and harvested its natural resources. They also exploited Africans as cheap labor for European companies.

France was eager to conquer western Africa. The United Kingdom already controlled much of eastern Africa. By building its own African empire, the French could limit the United Kingdom's power in Africa.

By 1890 French soldiers had driven well inland from Africa's western coast. Among other areas, France claimed Oubangui-Chari (modern Central African Republic). Throughout the 1890s, the French pushed northward into the Lake Chad Basin. They fought many battles with Fadlallah and Ouaddaï.

In 1898 and 1899, France linked three military expeditions to conquer the Lake Chad Basin and unify all French territories in western

This French drawing shows the French battling Fadlallah's forces in 1899. After losing this battle, the French defeated Fadlallah at the Battle of Kousséri.

Africa. The combined French forces finally defeated Fadlallah in 1900, at the Battle of Kousséri.

Shortly after this battle, France created the Military Territory of the Chad Countries and Protectorates. For the next several years, France struggled to subdue Chad's people. Ouaddaï, in particular, fiercely resisted colonization. Its forces constantly attacked French military posts.

Chad was the northernmost of a string of French territories extending from the central Sahara southwestward to the Atlantic Ocean. The other territories were Oubangui-Chari, Middle Congo (modern Republic of the Congo), and Gabon. In 1906 France merged Chad with Oubangui-Chari. Then, in 1910, France linked the three colonies in an alliance called French Equatorial Africa (better known by its

French acronym, AEF). The governor-general (highest-ranking colonial authority) in Brazzaville, Middle Congo, ruled over all AEF.

Over the next decade, France tightened its grip on Chad. French forces finally conquered Ouaddaï in 1912. In 1914 they occupied northern Chad. And in 1920, France separated Chad from Oubangui-Chari. Chad became AEF's fourth colony.

Colonial Chad

The French governor-general in Brazzaville controlled all four colonies' security matters, economic affairs, and communications with the government of France. In each AEF colony, a French lieutenant governor carried out the governor-general's orders. The governor-general tightly controlled his lieutenants.

However, Chad's lieutenant governor had a bit more freedom than his peers. Chad's capital at Fort-Lamy (modern N'Djamena) was so far from Brazzaville that AEF officials couldn't direct all its activities. Also, the French saw Chad mainly as a source of raw cotton and labor for use in its other AEF colonies, which were more productive.

France focused its meager development efforts in the south. It made plans for a local government of Chadian officials. It built a few schools for Chadian children. It let Christian missionaries (religious teachers) build schools there too. As a result, many southerners converted to Christianity. In 1929 France established cotton plantations (large farms for growing cash crops) throughout fertile southern Chad. It also built roads there to speed up shipping and travel.

French efforts in central Chad were weaker. This region was sparsely populated and less fertile. Since it wasn't likely to profit France, France didn't want to invest much money in it. The French placed only a thin government staff here. They built no roads or schools. They struggled to provide law and order. Though France had outlawed

SIMMERING TENSIONS

In 1924 France declared central Chad officially pacified (subdued). It then set about the task of building a colonial society in southern and central Chad. Though the French also occupied northern Chad, they never fully subdued the northern people. Nor did France try to build a national identity that included all Chad's ethnic groups.

Tensions simmered between northerners and southerners—as well as among Chad's many ethnic groups—as they had for thousands of years. These tensions helped lead to civil war and ongoing political instability after Chad gained independence from France.

Many French officials resisted working in poor, remote, and underdeveloped Chad. So government posts there were often punishments or fell to rookies. One expert on the French Empire concluded that it was impossible to be considered unfit for duty in Chad. No one was too crazy or too evil for an assignment there.

slavery, Arab raiders from this region kept terrorizing black Africans. The people of the Ouaddaï Highlands continued to resist French rule. France began to rely on force and on local chiefs to control this region.

France didn't even pretend to control northern Chad. The officers stationed there reached an unspoken agreement with Chad's Saharan people: as long as the caravan trails stayed reasonably safe and the people maintained minimal law and order, the French would leave the people alone. And for the most part, France did ignore northern Chad. It built no roads and no schools, established no local government, and did nothing to develop the economy. Its only major act in the region occurred in 1935. In that year, France negotiated a border adjustment with Italy, Libya's colonial ruler. The treaty (agreement) moved the Chad-Libya border about 62 miles (100 km) southward. But the French legislature never approved the treaty, so the border stayed put. The territory in question, called the Aozou Strip, became a source of conflict between Chad and Libya.

The French were never popular in the north, and they soon lost what little approval they'd earned in the south as well. Throughout the 1930s, the French uprooted villages to create cotton plantations and forced many Chadians to labor on public works. Thousands of Chadians died building a railway in Middle Congo. France demanded high yields from cotton farmers and bought cotton at very low prices. It heavily taxed Chadian households. Chadians resented these sorrows and hardships.

◉ Colonial Reforms

In 1939 Félix Éboué became Chad's lieutenant governor. Éboué was of mixed African and French ancestry. He was well educated and widely traveled. He'd served for decades in various French colonies.

Éboué saw that France's effort to build modern urban industries in its colonies was destroying African society. He proposed building rural industries instead, so families could stay put. He supported more and better education for Africans, which would help create an African middle class. He also supported returning power to traditional leaders.

During Éboué's first year in Chad, World War II (1939–1945) erupted in Europe. Germany and its allies (the Axis powers) fought a group of Allied nations, which included France and the United Kingdom (and

Félix Éboué (left) meets with Free French general Charles de Gaulle in Chad during World War II.

their colonies). In 1940 the Axis powers occupied northern France. It set up a puppet government, called Vichy France, to rule in the south as well as the occupied north. In the United Kingdom, a French general named Charles de Gaulle organized a resistance called Free France.

Éboué led AEF to support Free France. Chad became an important military base, and fifteen thousand Chadian soldiers joined the Free France cause. This support attracted international attention and money. Éboué became AEF's governor-general in 1941. He used his new power to promote reforms throughout AEF.

When Éboué died in 1944, Chad lost not only its key reformer but also his influence among the French. World War II ended one year later with an Allied victory. As France rebuilt its government, French voters rejected many of Éboué 's ideas. However, the 1946 French constitution did make some colonial reforms. It outlawed forced labor and introduced limited democracy (government by freely elected representatives). AEF's black Africans also became French citizens.

Though the status of Chad and its people had improved, real power over the colony remained in France. French staff continued to dominate AEF government. Another decade passed before the French offered higher education and civil service (government job) training to Chadians.

In 1956 the French legislature passed laws that expanded colonial voting rights. Two years later, AEF voters approved an act changing each territory from a colony to a separate country within the French Community. The French Community was a group of former colonies whose members controlled most of their own affairs. Many members, including Chad, used the French Community as a bridge to full national independence.

The Tombalbaye Regime

On August 11, 1960, Chad became a fully independent nation with the blessing of the French government. François Tombalbaye, the leader of the political party that controlled Chad's legislature at the time, became the nation's first president. Tombalbaye was a Christian and a member of the Sara people, southern Chad's dominant ethnic group.

Tombalbaye inherited leadership of a huge, harsh land that had weak infrastructure (roads and other public services), few resources, and a very diverse and poor population. Though France had drawn Chad's borders, it had done little to build economic, political, or cultural cooperation. Chadians needed a leader who could unify them and improve their lives.

But Tombalbaye didn't trust democracy. He banned all political parties except his own. He stripped the legislature's powers and filled high government positions with his supporters. He imprisoned or banished opponents and took power away from Muslim leaders. Soon he had complete command of Chad.

Tombalbaye's policies were biased. Southerners dominated the civil service and the army. Government workers and soldiers knew and cared little about northern culture. Southerners were also inexperienced. Northerners saw them as both arrogant and incompetent. Northerners viewed independence as simply a power shift from one enemy (the French) to another.

In the mid-1960s, Arab rebel groups began organizing throughout northern and central Chad, as well as in Libya and Sudan. Deadly riots erupted in central Chad in 1965. This year marked the beginning of a decades-long guerrilla war. (In a guerrilla war, an informal army fights against government troops, usually with harassment, sabotage, and terror.)

In 1968, with the conflict still raging, Tombalbaye asked France for military help. France said it would help only if Tombalbaye would reform his government. He grudgingly agreed. From 1969 to 1971, France sent troops to help Chad quell its rebellion. France also helped retrain Chad's army and civil service, end unpopular laws and taxes, and return some traditional powers to Muslim leaders. For these few years, Chad was fairly calm. The French began leaving in June 1971.

Two months later, Tombalbaye's reforms stopped. He criticized newly independent Libya's leader, Muammar al-Qaddafi, and began helping Libyan rebels. Qaddafi responded by helping Chadian rebels.

Chadian president **François Tombalbaye** *(right)* and French president Georges Pompidou ride through N'Djamena in the early 1970s.

The guerrilla war resurged. Then Tombalbaye suddenly changed his strategy. He cut off relations with Israel, which many Arab nations considered an enemy. This act attracted financial aid for Chad from Arab countries. It also reduced Arab support for Chad's rebels. The rebels began quarreling over their limited supplies, which weakened their efforts against Tombalbaye.

Tombalbaye's success was short-lived, though. He arrested suspected enemies. He ordered the army to round up workers for a massive cotton-planting effort. He began a program called Chaditude. The program forced people to change their names and changed place-names—especially those that were French—to African ones. He denounced Christianity and expelled missionaries. He executed civil servants and soldiers who refused to undergo *yondo*, a grueling and sometimes fatal Sara initiation rite that included scarring, brutal tests of stamina, beatings, and more. In response to these policies, Chadian military officers assassinated Tombalbaye on April 13, 1975.

Military Rule and Civil War

Most Chadians were glad to see the end of Tombalbaye's regime. They welcomed Chad's new military government and its leader, Colonel Félix Malloum. Malloum was a southerner, but he tried to draw northerners into his government. He ended many of Tombalbaye's hated policies and tried to govern fairly.

But Malloum's government soon lost favor. It failed to punish Tombalbaye's supporters for the crimes they'd committed. And it made little progress at unifying Chadians or coping with rebels. Libya increased its support for the rebels, and they steadily gained ground. Libya itself invaded Chad and took control of the Aozou Strip.

As Malloum lost popularity and territory, he began bargaining with the rebels. In late 1978, Malloum and rebel leader Hissène Habré formed a new shared government. This alliance lasted less than a year.

Hissène Habré

In early 1979, Habré used his rebel troops to oust Malloum and drive the Chadian army southward out of N'Djamena. Most of the city's Sara people followed. In the south, attacks against Muslims and northerners grew common. This violence spread into civil war among eleven armed factions.

Other African nations tried to control the chaos. They invited all the factions to a series of conferences in Nigeria. In late 1979, participants set up a cooperative government to rule until Chad could hold elections. Its top officers were Habré; another northern rebel leader, Goukouni Oueddei; and southerner Wadel Abdelkader Kamougué, one of Tombalbaye's assassins.

This alliance failed too. Within a year, Habré and Oueddei were at war again in northern and central Chad. Kamougué retreated to southern Chad, which had become a state within a state. Oueddei asked Libya for help. By late 1980, Libyan forces controlled northern and central Chad, including N'Djamena. Habré fled to Sudan.

Libya's intervention caused an international uproar. At that time, many countries saw Libya as a terrorist nation. Under intense foreign pressure, Oueddei asked Libya to leave. In late 1981, Libyan forces withdrew to the Aozou Strip.

Habré, Oueddei, and Kamougué were soon at war again. Habré emerged victorious. His forces took N'Djamena in June 1982. By year's end, they controlled all of Chad except the Tibesti Mountains, where Oueddei sought refuge. Kamougué fled the country.

▶ The Habré Era

Though Habré had seized Chad, violence continued there. Habré was a brutal dictator. He arrested, tortured, and killed thousands of suspected opponents. His government dealt with southern rebel groups by massacring them. His policies favored the Daza, his own ethnic group.

With Libyan support, Oueddei immediately formed a competing government in the north. In mid-1983, Libya's and Oueddei's troops reunited to attack Habré. They quickly conquered northern Chad.

Again, the world criticized Libya's interference. During the next year, France and other countries sent troops, weapons, and food to help Habré. Control of northern Chad changed hands several times. Eventually, Habré and Oueddei reached a deadlock.

In September 1984, France and Libya both agreed to leave Chad. By year's end, French troops were gone. Libyan troops remained, however. In 1985 Libya tightened its grip on northern Chad with more soldiers, tanks, and aircraft. It also built roads and a new airbase in Chad.

Meanwhile, Habré was reaching out to Oueddei and other rebel leaders. Gradually, all the rebels began fighting the Libyans along with Habré. With French and U.S. help, Chad finally expelled all the Libyan troops. In 1987 Chad and Libya signed a cease-fire agreement.

Chadian soldiers recover abandoned Libyan tanks after expelling Libyan troops in 1987.

The agreement held, despite minor skirmishes and Libya's continued claim on the Aozou Strip. Chad-Libya relations steadily improved over the next three years. In 1989 Habré and Qaddafi agreed to formally discuss their border and, if necessary, to settle their dispute in the United Nations (UN) International Court of Justice.

Though Chad had regained basic stability, ethnic tensions still simmered beneath the surface. In 1989 Habré accused his chief military adviser, Idriss Déby, of planning a coup (overthrow of the government). Déby, a member of the Zaghawa people, fled to Sudan. He rallied support among the Zaghawa of western Sudan and eastern Chad. Then, with additional help from other anti-Habré groups and from Libya, he began a series of attacks against Habré.

The Déby Regime

Idriss Déby

In December 1990, Déby's forces marched on N'Djamena and took over Chad. In February 1991, Déby's political movement founded a new government and named Déby president.

For the next five years, government troops and several rebel forces clashed violently, especially in the south. Many civilians died in the crossfire. Déby signed a truce with southern rebel groups in 1994, but unrest continued.

In 1996 Chadians approved a new constitution. Among other changes, the new constitution formally legalized opposing political parties. That year Chad also held its first multiparty presidential election. Legislative elections followed a few months later. Déby defeated Kamougué to win the presidency. Déby's party also won more than half the legislative seats. International observers noted serious voting flaws, such as voter intimidation and tampering with vote counts, but the results went unchallenged.

In the late 1990s, Déby's government signed more peace deals with various rebel groups. Skirmishes continued, but overall violence decreased. The government also secured a loan from the World Bank (a UN agency) to help develop Chad's economy. In 2000 Chad began drilling for oil in the south and building a pipeline to carry that oil through Cameroon to the Atlantic Ocean.

In 2001 Déby won a second presidential term. Observers again noted election flaws. Opposition parties accused the government of cheating. In response to these accusations, the government arrested six party leaders and killed one.

Civil war in western Sudan's Darfur region began spilling into Chad in 2003. Sudanese refugees fled Darfur by the thousands and sought refuge in eastern Chad. As related conflicts spread throughout the region, thousands of Chadians and Central Africans joined the Sudanese refugees.

Chad's oil began flowing in 2003. The terms of Chad's World Bank loan require Chad to spend most of its oil profits to develop its economy and relieve poverty. But despite this agreement, oil income has done little to improve the lives of ordinary Chadians.

Claiming that he was best qualified to handle Chad's many security, economic, and humanitarian problems, Déby changed Chad's constitution in mid-2005 to abolish presidential term and age limits. A public uproar followed. In 2005 several new Chadian rebel groups sprang up in Sudan. Chad and Sudan began accusing each other of backing and harboring rebels. In late 2005, Chad formally declared war on Sudan.

This photo shows a Sudanese refugee camp in Chad in 2004. Civil war in the Darfur region of Sudan forced thousands into neighboring Chad.

In 2006 Déby ran for president again. Opposition parties refused to participate, and Déby won the election.

As Déby, his political party, and the Zaghawa ethnic group kept a firm grip on Chad, violence and instability continued. Déby signed peace agreements with both Chadian rebels and the government of Sudan in 2006, but these agreements had little effect. Rebels attacked N'Djamena in 2006 and continued attacks in eastern Chad through 2007.

In February 2008, rebels attacked N'Djamena again. They surrounded Déby's palace, forced foreign embassy staff to evacuate, and delayed the arrival of a UN peacekeeping force. Government troops defeated the rebels, but more than one hundred people died in the fighting.

In March the UN force arrived and set about its job of protecting civilians and delivering humanitarian aid. The force reached full capacity in June, but Chad's condition remained fragile. By late 2008, more than a half million refugees were living in Chadian refugee camps, dependent on charity for survival. Chad and Sudan had cut off all ties with each other, and Chadian and Sudanese guerrilla groups were still fighting—with no end to the conflict in sight.

Residents of N'Djamena walk past a burned-out van in February 2008. The city bears many such scars of rebel-government fighting.

Visit www.vgsbooks.com for links to websites with up-to-date information on the ongoing struggles facing the people and government of Chad.

Government

Chadians govern their country by the constitution of 1996 (as revised in 2005). This document established a multiparty system with executive, legislative, and judicial branches.

The president leads Chad's executive branch. The president is both head of state (chief public representative) and effectively the head of government (chief decision-making authority). Citizens elect the president to a five-year term by popular vote. All adults eighteen years or older have the right to vote.

The president leads the country in cooperation with a prime minister, whom the president appoints. Ministers represent the various government departments. The president appoints these ministers as well as governors of the country's regions.

The national assembly is Chad's legislature. Its 155 members serve four-year terms. Chad's constitution requires local assemblies to pass laws for each region and its subdivisions, but no local elections have yet occurred.

A Supreme Court of appointed justices heads the judicial branch, which also includes courts of appeal, tribunals, and justices of the peace. The Constitutional Council reviews all laws and international treaties. The judicial system also includes a High Court of Justice. This is the only court that can try the president or ministers on criminal charges.

Chadians divide their land into eighteen regions. The regions are further divided into departments, sub-prefectures, and cantons.

THE PEOPLE

Chad is home to almost 11 million people. The population is growing about 3.1 percent per year. Researchers expect the population to exceed 29 million by 2050—an increase of 173 percent. This is one of the highest growth rates in the world. Like many other African nations, Chad has a young population. About 46 percent of Chadians are younger than fifteen years old.

Chad's government views its population growth rate as too high. To control this growth, the government created a national family planning agency in 1991. Soon thereafter, it legalized birth control, which French laws had banned in 1920. Despite these efforts, Chad's fertility rate remains high—about six children per woman.

Chad's population density is 22 people per square mile (8 people per sq. km). It's one of the world's least crowded nations overall. Chadians inhabit their country unevenly. About half the people live on just one-tenth of the land, in the far south. As a result, the northern population is very sparse. The population density of Chad's huge

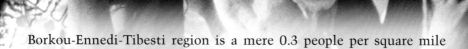

Borkou-Ennedi-Tibesti region is a mere 0.3 people per square mile (0.1 people per sq. km).

Though Chad's population has always been more rural than urban, that status is steadily changing. In 1960, when Chad became independent, 93 percent of Chadians lived in rural areas, while 7 percent lived in cities. Forty-five years later, only 75 percent of Chadians lived in rural areas, while 25 percent lived in cities. The number of urban dwellers continues to rise. Chad's decades of war have driven many rural refugees into the cities. Desertification and poverty are also pushing many farmers and herders to seek better lives in the cities. These migrants are swelling the cities and straining urban resources and services.

◉ Poverty

Chad is among the world's poorest countries. More than 54 percent of Chadians struggle to meet their basic food, clothing, and shelter needs.

Rural poverty is a major problem in Chad. Most people survive by farming, herding, or gathering forest products in southern and central Chad. Both drought and flooding are common here, and extreme weather often destroys crops and livestock. Widespread illiteracy (inability to read, write, and do simple math), large families, and ongoing unrest make it hard for many Chadians to improve their conditions.

Life in rural Chad is a constant struggle for survival. Poor nutrition is rampant. Due to chronic hunger, about 40 percent of Chadian children six years and younger are small for their age. Most families live in small homes in isolated villages. These households rarely have access to health care, education, clean drinking water, electricity, or sanitation. Drought and war have made it so hard to survive in Chad's countryside that entire families abandon their fields and villages to try their luck in the cities.

According to the UN Human Settlement Program, 99 percent of Chad's urban residents live in slums.

Cities offer more opportunity, but many newcomers find that conditions aren't much better there. Rural migrants often wind up in urban shantytowns. Shantytowns are settlements of poor people, usually on the outskirts of cities. Their homes are made of scrap material, and they often lack electricity, telephones, running water, or proper sanitation. Shantytowns tend to be overcrowded and suffer from high rates of crime and disease.

Health

As a result of widespread poverty, many Chadians suffer from hunger and live in substandard housing. Malnutrition and poor sanitation lead to many diseases and to early death. The average Chadian can expect to live only about forty-four years. Conditions that are rare or treatable in many other nations—such as malaria, tuberculosis, measles, polio, pneumonia, and cholera (a deadly diarrheal infection)—are common and deadly in Chad.

Acquired immunodeficiency syndrome (AIDS), a disease caused by the human immunodeficiency virus (HIV), is a growing problem in Chad. About 3.5 percent of Chadians between the ages of fifteen and forty-nine years carry HIV. This is among the highest HIV rates in the world. To hinder the spread of the virus, Chad has accepted international funds to establish a public HIV/AIDS education and treatment program. But resistance to speaking openly about sex, lack of health workers, poor infrastructure, and financial mismanagement have plagued this program. Chad's rate of infection continues to rise.

A Chadian baby receives medical treatment from a French military doctor. Chad's health-care system is unable to care for all of its people.

Very few Chadian women get adequate health care during pregnancy and childbirth. As a result, the nation's rates of infant mortality and maternal mortality are among the worst in the world. In Chad 114 out of every 1,000 babies die before the age of one year. For every 1,000 women in pregnancy or childbirth, 11 die.

Chad faces a pressing need for better public health systems, though the government is doing little to remedy the problems. These include not only safer drinking water and better sanitation but also more health-care workers and facilities. Chad has only four doctors for every one hundred thousand people. The cities of N'Djamena, Sarh, Moundou, Bongor, and Abéché have hospitals, but widely scattered clinics serve the rest of the country.

LIFE IN A REFUGEE CAMP

Conditions are desperate in refugee camps along Chad's southern and eastern borders. In these camps, more than five hundred thousand displaced Chadian, Sudanese, and Central African families live under plastic sheeting with meager food, water, sanitation, and medical care. Ten to fifty people per day may die in these camps, where more than one hundred people sometimes share one pit for a toilet.

Education

Under French rule, Chad had only a skeletal public education system. The colony built a few primary schools, but no secondary schools or universities. Instead, the French relied heavily on Christian missionaries to teach. Through the mid-1900s, mission schools were the only way for most people to learn basic skills. Illiteracy was high. About 90 percent of Chadian men and 99 percent of Chadian women couldn't read or write in any language.

After Chad won independence in 1960, its government began building a public education system and requiring children to attend primary school. Civil war, overcrowding, and insufficient staff and funding have plagued Chadian education ever since. Chad's literacy rates have risen steadily, but they're still among the world's lowest. In 2006 about 56 percent of males and 23 percent of females fifteen to twenty-four years old could read and write.

Chad requires children to attend six years of primary school. However, many Chadian children don't receive a full primary education. Families often keep girls at home to help with household tasks. Also, Chad does not have enough schools or qualified teachers. And although primary school is supposed to be free, it's not. Most schools require families to pay tuition fees. Nearly half of Chad's teachers get no government salaries. Parent-teacher associations pay the salaries instead.

About 92 percent of boys and 62 percent of girls enroll in primary

RELIGIOUS EDUCATION

Chad's poor public education system prompts many Muslim families to turn to Islamic schools instead *(below)*. Most large towns have one or two private religious schools (usually Islamic). Governments, charities, and individuals from Middle Eastern countries such as Saudi Arabia, Egypt, and Libya typically fund these schools. Egyptian teachers staff many of them.

school. Teachers instruct in both French and Arabic, Chad's two official languages. The average primary school has one teacher per seventy students. At the end of the sixth primary year, all children take a national exam.

Those who pass the exam may attend any of a variety of secondary schools. These secondary schools offer different types of education, such as university preparation, teacher training, technical and scientific education, and vocational training. Schools teach in either French or Arabic.

About 23 percent of boys and 8 percent of girls enroll in secondary school. Secondary schooling lasts seven years. At the end of professional schooling, students earn certificates qualifying them to work in various careers. At the end of university preparation, students take a national exam. Those who pass the exam may proceed to higher education.

University education is available at two institutions. The University of N'Djamena offers a full array of undergraduate programs in the humanities and sciences, as well as graduate programs in law, medicine, economics, biology, history, geography, and Arabic literature. King Faisal University, also in N'Djamena, is an Islamic institution founded by the Kingdom of Saudi Arabia. It primarily trains Arabic-speaking professors and administrators for positions at Arabic schools in Chad.

⊙ Ethnic Groups

Chad is home to about two hundred ethnic groups. The exact population numbers for the various groups is difficult to estimate, since many groups overlap and Chad actually avoids tracking ethnic statistics.

This great variety is a result of Chad's location. Chad lies at a crossroads between northern Africa, where most people are Arabs, and the central continent, where most people are black Africans. For thousands of years, different peoples have settled in various parts of Chad. But they haven't necessarily stayed put. Chad's open terrain, rainfall patterns, and low population density have encouraged people to move around. Slave trading and French colonization complicated the ethnic patchwork.

The lines dividing Chadian ethnic groups are blurry. Many groups share traits—such as language, ancestry, or territory—with others. For example, nearly all Chadian ethnic groups organize their societies around clans (large family groups whose members share a key ancestor). And ethnic similarities and differences continue to shift, just as they have for centuries. Nonetheless, Chad's ethnic groups generally belong to three large categories: nomads of the Sahara zone, seminomads of the Sahel zone, and farmers of the Sudan zone.

The Toubou dominate Chad's Sahara. This Arab people most likely originated in the Nile River valley to the east. They live mainly in northern Chad but also in Libya, Niger, and Sudan. Most Toubou people live around the Tibesti Mountains as nomadic or seminomadic herders. Each Toubou clan claims certain oases, pastures, and wells. The Toubou divide themselves into two large subgroups, the Teda and the Daza. They are mainly Muslim.

The Toubou live in the Tibesti Mountains in northern Chad. *Inset:* A Toubou boy

 Visit www.vgsbooks.com for links to websites with more information on the people of Chad. Discover what international organizations are doing to help the people of Chad.

The people of central Chad are diverse. The ethnic groups in this region are of Arab or mixed Arab and black African ancestry. Most are Muslim. In the northern Sahel, societies tend to be seminomadic. In the southern Sahel, they're generally settled. The Maba dominate the Ouaddaï Highlands. These are the same people who founded the Ouaddaï Kingdom. The Kanembu and Tunjur people, both Arab groups, live northeast of Lake Chad. The Kanembu were the people of the Kanem-Bornu Empire. The Yedina and the Kuri inhabit the Lake Chad region. Farther south live the Barma, who founded the Baguirmi Kingdom, as well as the Hausa and the Fulani, who originated west of Lake Chad. The Kotoko, descendants of the Sao civilization, live along the northern Logone and Chari rivers. On and around the Guéra Massif live the Hadjeray, the Bulala, the Kuka, and the Midogo.

The Sara people dominate southern Chad. They are also the largest ethnic group overall. They too claim descent from the Sao. Surrounding the Sara are many smaller ethnic groups, such as the Laka, the Mbum, the Gula, the Tumak, and the Tangale. Most southerners are settled farmers of black African descent. These people typically practice animism, Christianity, or a combination of the two religions.

STRONG WOMEN

Although the country's laws forbid gender discrimination, it happens anyway. Females get far less education and have limited job opportunities. They marry young—sometimes at eleven or twelve and nearly always by the age of eighteen. Nearly 40 percent of Chadian women live in polygamous households, where one husband has two or more wives. Domestic violence is common. In property and inheritance disputes, local customs favor men. Chadian women in refugee camps are especially vulnerable. Many of them have no idea whether their husbands, fathers, and brothers are alive or dead. These women often suffer rape and sexual abuse.

Despite all these disadvantages, Chadian women display amazing strength. They do most of the strenuous farmwork and housework. They provide and care for large families, often on their own. In refugee camps, they organize to teach better hygiene, to provide better security, to build community, and to share their meager resources. With sheer determination, women are holding together the tattered fabric of Chad's society.

CULTURAL LIFE

Because Chad is so isolated and so arid, outsiders sometimes call it the dead heart of Africa. But at the heart of Africa, where hundreds of ethnic groups meet and mingle, cultural life throbs with complex rhythms.

▶ Religion

Chad has no official religion. About 53 percent of Chadians are Muslim. About 34 percent are Christian, and about 7 percent practice traditional African religions (animism). Of the remaining 6 percent, half follow other religions and half are atheists (do not believe in any god). These figures mask the impact of animism on Chad's culture. Many Chadians blend Islam or Christianity with animist beliefs. This blending is called syncretism.

Islam means "surrender to the will of Allah" in the Arabic language. *Allah* is the word for "God." Muslims believe that Allah gave messages to his prophet Muhammad through the angel Gabriel. The holy scriptures of the Quran contain these messages.

Muslims strive to fulfill the five pillars (central duties) of Islam: declaring faith in Allah and Muhammad; praying five times daily; giving charity; fasting from sunrise to sunset during the holy month of Ramadan; and traveling to the holy city of Mecca once in a lifetime, if possible. Friday is the day of worship for Muslims. Men go to the mosque to learn and pray. Women pray at home or in separate parts of the mosque.

Christianity is Chad's newest religion. It arrived in the early 1900s, when Christian missionaries began working in Chad. Many Chadians found Christianity unappealing. Missionaries often forbade dancing, drinking alcohol, and practicing local customs. But the missionaries' social work was very appealing. They set up schools, clinics, and hospitals long before the colonial government did. Throughout the 1900s, these facilities provided most of the education and health care Chadians received. Missionaries attracted Chadian supporters by caring for Chadian minds and bodies.

A Chadian Catholic priest celebrates Mass in N'Djamena. Many Chadian Christians retain elements of animism.

Animism is Chad's oldest religion. Animism as a chief religion is most prevalent in the south. Animism's central belief is that spirits live in all things—people, animals, plants, and the natural world. It also teaches that dead ancestors are spiritually alive. Spirits may be good or evil, and they can affect human lives and events. For animists, keeping the spirits in balance is very important.

Animism offers a way to deal with practical problems. For example, many Chadians believe that spirits cause certain illnesses and that only a shaman (spiritual healer) can determine which spirit has caused a particular problem. A shaman may prescribe rituals or herbal remedies to lure a problematic spirit from someone's body. Or a shaman may hold a ritual to ask ancestor spirits for help. Specific rituals and beliefs vary among Chad's many ethnic groups.

◉ Language

Chad's official languages are Chadian Arabic (a local dialect of the Arabic language) and French.

Learn a few simple phrases in Chad's two official languages: Chadian Arabic and French.

English	Chadian Arabic	French
hello	salaam aleekum	bonjour
how are you (to a man)	keefak	comment allez-vous
how are you (to a woman)	keefik	comment allez-vous
thank you	shukraan	merci

Both languages appear in government documents and media. Chadian Arabic is the first language of about 750,000 citizens. It serves many more as a second language, making it the most widely spoken tongue in the country. French is the first language of about 3,000 Chadians—most of them members of Chad's small upper class.

Many peoples speak local languages in addition to one or both of the two official languages. All told, the people of Chad speak more than 130 different languages. Chad's languages represent three of Africa's major language families: Nilo-Saharan, Afroasiatic, and Niger-Congo.

This hospital sign uses both Chadian Arabic and French, the two official languages of Chad.

Literature

Chad has a long, rich tradition of oral, or spoken, literature. For many centuries, villagers have listened to storytellers at births, weddings, funerals, and other community events. Oral literature still thrives in Chad. Each ethnic group has a unique literary tradition. These traditions include historical narratives, folktales, legends, proverbs, and ritual drama.

Some modern Chadian writers work in Arabic, but most work in French. The modern Chadian literary scene is more vibrant in France than in Chad. Many educated Chadians live in France, where more people are able to publish and buy books.

Joseph Brahim Seïd is a writer and politician. He served as Chad's minister of justice from 1966 to 1975. He's famous for his novels *Au Tchad sous les étoiles* (In Chad under the stars) and *Un enfant du Tchad* (A child of Chad), both based on his own life.

Mahamet "Baba" Moustapha was a playwright. His satires question the value of urbanization, denounce dictators, and criticize worn-out traditions. *Le Commandant Chaka* (Commander Chaka) is his most famous play.

Mahamat-Saleh Haroun is a Chadian film director who lives and works in France. His autobiographical feature *Bye Bye Africa* has won several international film awards. Chad itself does not have much of a film industry.

Antoine Bangui-Rombaye is a political writer. He served in President Tombalbaye's government until he had a disagreement with Tombalbaye. The president threw him in prison, claiming that he had planned a coup. His book *Prisonnier de Tombalbaye* (Prisoner of Tombalbaye) describes his ordeal there. He has also published an autobiography and a scathing critique of President Déby.

Koulsy Lamko is a Chadian playwright, poet, novelist, and scholar. He has spent much of his career developing and promoting community theater in Africa. His experience among Rwandans recovering from their nation's 1994 genocide (a mass murder of nearly one million Rwandans) inspired him to write his only novel, *La phalène des collines* (The butterfly of the hills).

Music and Dance

Chad has a vibrant traditional music and dance scene. Each of Chad's many ethnic groups has a unique tradition of music and dance.

In the south, Sara music uses the *balafon* (a large wooden xylophone), the *kinde* (a five-string bow harp), the *kodjo* (a large drum), and whistles. Barma music features drums and zithers (plucked string instruments). The Barma are also famous for a dance in which participants carry out a mock battle with large clubs.

In the Sahel, the Fulani people play single-reed flutes. Kanembu music combines flutes and drums. The Hausa people mark their most important ceremonies by playing the *kakaki*, a 10-foot (3 m) tin trumpet.

In the Sahara, the Teda people play lutes and fiddles. Men use the *keleli* (a kind of lute) to "speak" for them, as Teda culture frowns on men singing in front of women. Women, however, may sing for men. The Teda are also known for belly dancing.

Chadians enjoy popular music as well. Modern Chadian music began when the band Chari Jazz formed in 1964. Many bands have followed. Popular musical styles in Chad include soukous (fast dance music that combines African, Caribbean, and South American sounds) and *sai* (an upbeat dance music from southern Chad). The band Tibesti is one of Chad's most popular modern musical groups. This band mixes sai with rap, rock, and reggae.

Food

Chad's staple foods are millet and sorghum. Cooks may boil these grains or grind them into flour. People use the flour to make bread, porridge, pancakes, or a paste rolled into balls. Dipping sauces and

stews accompany the grains. The stews and sauces contain herbs, spices, and vegetables such as onions, okra, peanuts, and tomatoes. Cooks add meat or fish when they can afford them.

A woman cooks outside of her home.

Other important foods in Chad are cassava (a starchy root), potatoes, and legumes, such as lentils. Beef, chicken, and mutton (sheep meat) are widely available to those who can afford them. Common vegetables are cassava leaves, carrots, green beans, okra, onions, and squash. Fruits such as dates and citrus are popular too. Sesame seeds provide oil and flavoring for many Chadian dishes.

Chadian cuisine varies by region. In the north, people eat more meat, dairy, dates, and raisins. Near Chad's lakes and rivers, fish such as Nile perch, catfish, eel, tilapia, and carp are popular foods. Chadians preserve fish by drying, salting, or smoking it. In the south, people eat a wide variety of fruits, such as bananas, mangoes, melons, guavas, papayas, and pineapples.

Chadians eat their main meal in the evening. It's served on a large plate set on a mat on the ground. People sit around the plate. Men and women usually eat separately. Popular snacks are peanuts (raw or roasted), corn (roasted or boiled), and *fangasou* (similar to doughnuts). In the cities, many street vendors sell baguettes (French bread) and shish kebabs (skewered roasted meat).

Tea is the most common drink in Chad. *Karkanji*, a sweet red tea made from dried hibiscus flowers, is very popular. Fruit juices and locally made soft drinks are also common. Muslims do not drink alcohol, but adult non-Muslims in the south enjoy millet beer and liquor.

Chadians typically eat their main meal seated on the ground around the main dish.

KARKANJI

Hot, thirsty Chadians love karkanji because it's refreshing and cheap. People can make it entirely with plants grown in Chad. You can try a version of this tea.

1 gallon water

1½ cups dried hibiscus flowers (available at health-food stores)

½ cup gingerroot (peeled and sliced)

1½ cups sugar (or to taste)

1. Pour water into a large pot. Add hibiscus flowers and gingerroot.
2. Place the pot on the stove, turn heat to high, and bring the mixture to a full rolling boil.
3. Cover the pot, lower the heat, and let the mixture simmer for 10 minutes.
4. Add sugar according to taste. Mix until the sugar dissolves. Simmer mixture for 5 more minutes.
5. Remove from heat and let cool for at least 1 hour.
6. Add ice and serve. Serves 8.

Art and Architecture

Chad's most famous art is its Saharan rock art. For about six thousand years, the people of northern Chad carved and painted pictures of humans and animals on the rocks of the Tibesti Mountains and the Ennedi Plateau. This art evolved through many styles, recording Chad's changing society. This type of art declined as Islam spread throughout Chad.

Most contemporary Chadian artisans create works either for their own use or for sale to tourists. Weavers make baskets, mats, and fans decorated with violet and green dyes. Potters make water jars and other containers that keep their contents cool even in hot weather. Other artisans weave rugs, make jewelry, tool leather, carve wood, or engrave gourds. Each ethnic group has distinct ways of shaping and decorating its crafts.

Few Chadians practice modern graphic arts. Those who do generally live and work in N'Djamena. The government maintains the capital's National Museum but does not otherwise support the arts.

Architectural preservation and innovation are both rare in Chad. A few palaces, mosques, churches, and other buildings from Chad's

These circular huts are the **traditional homes** of farmers in southern Chad.

various empires survive—especially in Abéché. But most architectural treasures lie in ruins from war or neglect.

Many southern farmers build traditional homes—circular buildings with adobe (sun-dried earth) walls and conical straw roofs. Herders in the north often live in tents. However, plain concrete-and-iron buildings are common throughout the country.

Sports and Recreation

Chad's most popular sport is soccer (called football outside the United States). Many Chadians avidly follow Sao, the national soccer team. Several Chadian soccer players have played for French teams. Basketball, boxing, and martial arts are popular in the cities. Chad's excellent track-and-field athletes have a large following too. Chadian sprinter Kaltouma Nadjina competed at the Olympic Games in both Sydney, Australia (2000), and Athens, Greece (2004). In the 2008 Beijing, China, Olympic games, sprinter Moumi Sebergue competed in the men's 100 meters.

Chadians throughout the country enjoy freestyle wrestling. Matches often take place when two groups meet to water their cattle.

Participants from the two groups pair off by age. Before they start wrestling, they traditionally don animal hides and cover themselves with dust.

Boys play soccer whenever they can. Chadian girls play *tap tap* (a type of hopscotch) and jump rope. Both girls and boys play hide-and-seek and make toys out of everyday objects. They like to roll wheels and tires around with sticks. Boys sometimes carry slingshots, which they use to hunt small birds.

Chadians of all ages enjoy board games. They usually play on the ground, not on a game board. One favorite is mancala, a game that's popular throughout Africa. Mancala players move stones or dried beans around two rows of six cups on a board or scooped into the ground. The object is to capture all the opponent's pieces. Another favorite is war, a chesslike game involving twenty sticks on a grid of twenty-five squares. Both games demand careful strategy and good math skills.

Visit www.vgsbooks.com for links to websites with additional information on Chadian culture, including holidays, foods, sports, and games.

Holidays and Festivals

Chad's national holidays begin with New Year's Day on January 1. On March 8, Chadians celebrate International Women's Day with parades and other special events. Labor Day is May 1. Independence Day (August 11) brings military parades, speeches, and flag ceremonies. November 28 celebrates Chad's proclamation as a republic. Chadians also honor the current government's ascent to power on Freedom and Democracy Day. This date changes with each government. Under Déby the holiday falls on December 1.

Chad's people also celebrate Christian and Muslim religious holidays. The most important Christian holidays are Easter (date varies), All Saints' Day (November 1), and Christmas (December 25). Muslim holidays follow a lunar calendar, so their dates change each year. The most important holiday, Eid al-Fitr, happens at the end of the holy month of Ramadan. During the daylight hours of Ramadan, Muslims avoid eating and drinking to honor Allah's revelation of the Quran to Muhammad. On Eid al-Fitr, Muslims celebrate with feasting, praying, and family gatherings. Other key Muslim holidays are Eid al-Adha, which honors Abraham's willingness to sacrifice his son to God, and Eid al-Mawlid, which celebrates Muhammad's birth.

THE ECONOMY

Chad's geographic isolation, rugged terrain, and harsh climate have hampered economic development. Decades of war have also held the country back. Corruption, lack of roads, and outdated technology pose other obstacles. These challenges make Chad one of the poorest and least developed countries in the world. Its average annual income per person is only about $250—a figure that ranks among the world's lowest. More than 54 percent of Chadians live in extreme poverty.

The government is trying to expand Chad's economy. Chadians rely heavily on farming for their survival. But in Chad, where droughts are severe and frequent and where insects can destroy an entire harvest in a matter of days, farming is risky. The government hopes that introducing new types of businesses will offer some protection from this risk.

◉ Industry

Chad's industrial sector includes energy, manufacturing, and mining. This sector is responsible for about 50 percent of the nation's gross

domestic product (GDP). (The GDP is the total value of goods and services produced inside the country in a year.) Industry, combined with
services, employs about 20 percent of the nation's labor force.

Oil production is responsible for nearly all Chad's industrial revenue. In the 1970s, scientists found vast oil reserves in southern
Chad. But for many years, Chad's unstable governments couldn't tap
this resource. In 2000 Chad finally began drilling for oil and building
a pipeline to carry that oil through Cameroon to the Atlantic Ocean.
The oil started flowing in 2003. Since then Chad has become the
tenth-largest oil producer in Africa.

Chad funds its oil exploration, drilling, and transport through a loan
from the World Bank. The terms of this loan require Chad to use 70
percent of its oil profits for programs that improve health, education,
agriculture, infrastructure, environment, rural development, safety,
and good governance. However, oil income has not yet improved the
lives of ordinary Chadians. Chad experienced an immediate oil boom

for two years, but the government spent a large chunk of that income on defense. The World Bank responded by freezing Chad's funds. The two parties worked out their differences in 2006. But since then, Chad's oil production has slowed dramatically—and so have oil profits meant for the public good.

Chadians use none of their country's oil. Chad has no oil refineries, no coal or natural gas deposits, and no hydroelectric or solar power projects. So Chadians must import refined oil from Nigeria and Cameroon to supply their commercial energy needs. Chad generates and consumes tiny amounts of electricity. Only 2 percent of Chadians have electrical service. Most Chadians burn animal dung or wood instead.

Manufacturing contributes a small portion of Chad's industrial revenue. Chadian factories lie mainly in the south or in N'Djamena, and most of them process farm products. Factories that process raw cotton, make cotton cloth, or produce cottonseed soap and oil are the most numerous. Several towns in southern and central Chad have meat-processing and meat-packing plants. Other factories make beer or cigarettes or process sugarcane or natron.

Chadians work on an oil rig in southern Chad. The discovery of oil has brought hope for Chad's economic future.

Mining is responsible for an even smaller part of Chadian industry. Although mining for nonmetal minerals (natron, kaolin, limestone, salt, sand, stone, and gravel) is active, it's not profitable. Strife has largely prevented Chad from exploiting its more valuable minerals (uranium, gold, tungsten, tin, bauxite, silver, iron ore, titanium, and diamonds).

◗ Services

Chad's service sector refers to all business activity that provides useful labor instead of material goods. This sector includes banking, transportation, wholesale and retail trade, business services, telecommunications, hotels, bars, restaurants, tourism, construction, and government services. This sector is responsible for about 29 percent of the nation's GDP. Combined with industry, it employs about 20 percent of the workforce.

Chad's service sector includes many informal businesses. Because informal businesses are hard to measure, they probably contribute more to Chadian livelihoods than the official statistics suggest. Many people sell goods, provide everyday services, and conduct trade without formal structure, organized accounting, or government permits. They want to avoid the high taxes Chad demands from registered businesses. Informal commerce ranges from individual street vendors peddling food and household wares to mechanics and repair people to companies that ship tons of gum arabic (acacia tree sap) out of the country.

Government services, foreign trade, and construction are responsible for most of Chad's official service revenue. These businesses are growing steadily to support Chad's oil industry. Construction of roads, power stations, buildings, and communications facilities has been active in the twenty-first century. Financial and commercial services are growing too. Oil income, in turn, is funding the growth of government poverty-relief programs.

Tourism-related services contribute little to Chad's economy. Prolonged violence frightens away visitors. However, Chad's stark beauty, fascinating wildlife, and diverse cultures do draw some adventurous travelers. The main destination of most tourists is Zakouma National Park in southern Chad.

◗ Agriculture

Chad's agricultural sector includes farming, fishing, and forestry. This sector is responsible for about 21 percent of the nation's GDP. It employs about 80 percent of Chadian workers.

Most of these people live and work on small farms. The farms produce staple foods such as sorghum, millet, cassava, potatoes, and legumes as well as cash crops such as cotton and sugarcane. The wet, fertile Sudan zone is the most productive farming region. The Sahel and Sahara zones are drier and less fertile. These regions mainly support livestock such as beef and dairy cattle, poultry, sheep, and goats. Cotton and meat are key exports.

Along Chad's lakes and rivers, fishing is an important agricultural activity. Fishing families harvest Nile perch, catfish, eel, tilapia, and carp. However, drought and excessive irrigation are shrinking Lake Chad and draining the country's rivers. Many Chadians who once relied on fishing are turning to farming for survival.

Forestry is another important part of Chad's agricultural sector. Although Chad has no large forests, wooded areas cover about 25 percent of its land. Wood supplies about 98 percent of the energy Chadians use (imported oil supplies the other 2 percent). The country's acacia trees produce hundreds of tons of gum arabic per year.

Foreign Trade

Like other areas of Chad's economy, foreign trade has grown alongside Chad's oil industry. For many decades, Chad imported far more goods and services than it exported. That changed in 2003, when Chad began exporting oil. Since then Chad's balance of foreign trade has reversed.

Chad's export trade relies on just a few products. Oil accounts for 92 percent of exports. Cotton and related products, livestock, and gum arabic make up the remaining 8 percent. Nearly 80 percent of Chadian

BY GUM

Chadian workers handpick solid chunks of sap from acacia trees. It's scratchy, prickly work because the trees are covered with sharp thorns. Chadian companies send the raw sap to Europe for processing. Factories around the world then use it to make ink, adhesives, medicine, cosmetics, soft drinks, chewing gum, and candy.

Gum arabic is a natural emulsifier. That means it can hold together substances that normally wouldn't mix well. It's also nontoxic and edible. In soda, gum arabic keeps sugar from settling to the bottom of the drink. Drug companies use the gum to prevent medicine ingredients from separating. On postage stamps, gum arabic is a handy, lickable adhesive. Printers use it to make ink more permanent and to protect metal printing plates.

Humans have been using this valuable sap for thousands of years. In ancient Egypt, gum arabic was essential to making mummies. Artists have also used it as a paint binder since biblical times.

goods end up in the United States. China, South Korea, and European nations buy the remaining 20 percent.

Chad imports transportation machinery and equipment, chemicals, refined oil, noncotton textiles (yarn and cloth), and food. Food imports vary from year to year, depending on weather and other environmental factors. About 65 percent of Chadian imports come from Europe—mainly France but also Germany and Belgium. The remaining 35 percent of imports come from Cameroon, Nigeria, the United States, and Saudi Arabia.

⊙ Transportation

Chad's transportation system is underdeveloped. Poor infrastructure hinders the nation's economy. But Chad is using oil income and foreign aid to improve the quality and number of its roads and airports.

Chad's network of roads is sparse and unreliable. It has about 20,754 miles (33,400 km) of roads in total. Less than 1 percent of these roads are paved. Most of the roads lie in the south. They're often impassable during the rainy season. In the north, roads are mere tracks across the desert. Horses, donkeys, and camels are the most reliable forms of transportation throughout much of Chad.

Chad has fifty-five airports. Seven have paved runways. The largest facility is N'Djamena International Airport. Toumaï Air Tchad,

Chadians in the Sahara often depend on **overcrowded trucks** for transportation between towns.

Chad's national airline, flies between major Chadian cities and to other African destinations.

About 1,243 miles (2,000 km) of the Chari and Logone rivers are navigable, but only during the rainy season. Chad has no railways.

Communications

A lack of electricity limits Chad's communication services. Few households own telephones. The nation has only about 13,000 land lines. Cellular phones are more common but still not widespread. Chadians own about 466,000 mobile phones. Few private homes have computers or Internet access. However, both are available to city dwellers via Internet cafés and hotels, where users can rent computer time. Chad has about sixty thousand Internet users.

Chad's constitution permits freedom of expression. But the government restricts this right. It frequently harasses, fines, and arrests journalists who criticize the state. It accuses them of libel (spreading damaging lies), which is a crime in Chad. The nation's High Council of Communication (HCC) has the power to stop publications and broadcasts for libel. Also, Chad's longstanding ethnic tensions make many subjects off-limits to the press.

Nevertheless, newspapers that criticize the government circulate freely in the cities. They have little influence because so many Chadians live in the country or can't read—or both.

Radio is Chad's most popular form of mass media. Despite high licensing fees, the country has thirteen privately owned stations. The government keeps a close eye on these stations. If they grow too critical or fail to pay their fees, the state threatens to shut them down. Chad has only one television station, Teletchad. The government owns it, so its news coverage is biased.

The Future

Chad faces many pressing economic and social challenges. In order to reduce poverty and improve the lives of its growing population, Chad must strengthen and expand virtually every sector of its economy and infrastructure.

To meet these challenges, Chad needs money—and lots of it. Oil offers great income potential for Chad. It may help the country become financially self-sufficient. Chad hopes to produce energy for its own use too. In 2007 Chad signed a deal with a Chinese company to

Visit www.vgsbooks.com for links to websites with current information on the state of the Chadian economy.

build a Chadian oil refinery. Energy independence could improve Chad's economy and standard of living in many ways.

But before Chad can realize this potential, it requires something even more basic: peace. Chad is an ancient land with many centuries of struggle behind it. Even so, the late twentieth and early twenty-first centuries have proven to be some of Chad's most difficult years. Several decades of war, drought, and political turmoil have made the already hard lives of Chadians nearly unbearable.

Chadians have shown over and over that they can survive in a harsh environment and rebuild when disaster—natural or human—strikes. Chad's problems will not be easy to solve. But with wise use of its valuable resources, as well as help from international peacekeepers and aid organizations, Chad has high hopes for a brighter future.

SOLAR COOKERS

Nearly eighteen thousand people live in the Iridimi refugee camp in eastern Chad. These people traditionally use firewood for cooking. But wood is scarce in Iridimi, so women and girls must travel far outside the camp to find it. Many of them have suffered violent attacks at the hands of bandits, rebel soldiers, and local villagers who resent having to share their resources.

Since 2005, aid organizations have teamed up to provide more than fifteen thousand low-cost solar cookers *(below)* to the Iridimi refugees. These cookers are made of cardboard and aluminum foil folded into a basket shape. A cooking pot rests in the center of the basket. Each family gets at least two cookers. The project has been a huge success. Many are using the cookers. Health, safety, and air quality are better too. Trips outside the camp have dropped 86 percent. Violent assaults have all but disappeared.

Timeline

CA. 7,000,000 B.C. The world's oldest known hominid lives in Chad's Djourab Desert.

CA. 10,000 B.C. Early humans settle along the shores of Lake Chad. They leave behind tools, pottery, and rock paintings.

CA. 1000 B.C. Human settlements spread south of Lake Chad.

CA. A.D. 500 The towns south of Lake Chad form the Sao civilization.

600s-800s The Sao civilization peaks. Nomads from the north and east settle in the region. Many small chiefdoms emerge.

800s Chad's chiefdoms merge into larger kingdoms. The Kanem Empire, ruled by the Duguwa dynasty, emerges on Lake Chad's northeastern shore.

900s Arab migrants and traders introduce Islam to Chad.

MID-1200s The Kanem Empire peaks under Mai Dunama Dabbalemi.

LATE 1300s Internal power struggles and external attacks tear Kanem apart.

CA. 1400 The Sayfawa dynasty is forced out of its capital. The people of Kanem move to Bornu. The kingdom becomes known as Kanem-Bornu.

1522 The Baguirmi Kingdom emerges southeast of Kanem-Bornu.

1635 The Ouaddaï Kingdom emerges east of Kanem-Bornu.

MID-1600s Baguirmi breaks free of Kanem-Bornu and begins expanding.

EARLY 1800s A new Saharan trade route links Ouaddaï with Benghazi on the Mediterranean Sea. Ouaddaï grows powerful. It conquers Baguirmi and eastern Kanem-Bornu.

1892-1893 The Sudanese warlord Rabih Fadlallah conquers Baguirmi and what's left of Kanem-Bornu.

1890s The French advance into the Lake Chad Basin.

1900 French forces defeat Fadlallah at the Battle of Kousséri. France creates the Military Territory of Chad.

1910 France creates a huge colonial alliance called French Equatorial Africa (AEF), which includes the territory of Chad.

1912-1914 French forces finally conquer Ouaddaï and occupy Chad's Sahara zone.

1920 Chad becomes a separate colony within AEF.

1935 France and Italy negotiate a border adjustment between Chad and Libya. The deal fails, creating a conflict zone called the Aozou Strip.

1939-1945   Chad supports Free France in World War II.

1946   A new French constitution outlaws forced labor and intro-
duces limited democracy. Chadians become French citizens.

1958   Chad becomes a separate country within the French Community.

1960   Chad gains full independence on August 11. François Tombalbaye
becomes the first president.

1965   Deadly riots erupt in central Chad. A decades-long conflict begins—at first
between northerners and southerners but eventually splintering to involve
many Chadian ethnic groups as well as France, Libya, and Sudan.

1975   Chadian military officers assassinate Tombalbaye. Colonel Félix Malloum
leads a new military government.

1979   Hissène Habré ousts Malloum.

1980-1981   Alliances and control of various zones changes hands many times among Habré,
Goukouni Oueddei, Wadel Abdelkader Kamougué, and Muammar al-Qaddafi.

1982   Habré regains control over most of Chad. Oueddei forms a competing government in the Tibesti Mountains.

MID-1980s   Habré (backed by France) and Oueddei (backed by Libya) struggle for control of
northern Chad. Libya tightens its grip on northern Chad.

LATE 1980s   Chadian rebel groups expel the Libyans with French and U.S. help.

1990   Idriss Déby overthrows Habré.

1996   Chadian voters approve a new constitution. Chad also holds its first multiparty
elections. Déby and his party maintain power, despite flawed elections.

2000   Chad begins drilling for oil.

2003   Sudanese civil war spills into Chad. Related conflicts spread throughout the
region. Chadian oil begins flowing.

2005   Déby changes Chad's constitution to abolish presidential term and
age limits. A public uproar follows, and several new Chadian rebel
groups spring up in Sudan. Chad-Sudan relations deteriorate until Chad
declares war on Sudan.

2006   Déby and his party win another flawed election. Rebels attack
N'Djamena unsuccessfully.

2006-2007   Déby, Chadian rebels, and Sudan sign peace agreements, but they
have little effect.

2008   Rebels attack N'Djamena and fail again. Chad and Sudan
cut off all ties. UN peacekeepers arrive. The refugee
population exceeds a half million people.

COUNTRY NAME Republic of Chad

AREA 495,755 square miles (1,284,000 sq. km)

MAIN LANDFORMS Lake Chad Basin, Tibesti Mountains, Ennedi Plateau, Ouaddaï Highlands, Guéra Massif, Sahara

HIGHEST POINT Emi Koussi, 11,204 feet (3,415 m) above sea level

LOWEST POINT Djourab Depression, 525 feet (160 m) above sea level

MAJOR RIVERS Chari River, Logone River

ANIMALS African wildcats, antelopes, Barbary sheep, bee-eaters, bustards, camels, Cape buffalo, cheetahs, cranes, desert locusts, elephants, foxes, freshwater manatees, giraffes, hippos, hyenas, jackals, Kuri cattle, leopards, lions, Nile crocodiles, ostriches, otters, rhinoceroses

CAPITAL CITY N'Djamena

OTHER MAJOR CITIES Moundou, Sarh, Abéché

OFFICIAL LANGUAGES Chadian Arabic and French

MONETARY UNIT CFA franc. 100 centimes = 1 franc.

CHADIAN CURRENCY

The official currency of the Chad is the CFA franc. CFA stands for *coopération financière en Afrique centrale*, or "financial cooperation in Central Africa." The CFA franc is also the currency in the neighboring countries of Cameroon, Central African Republic, Republic of the Congo, Equatorial Guinea, and Gabon.

The franc is divided into 100 centimes. Banknotes include denominations of 500, 1,000, 2,000, 5,000, and 10,000, while coins have demoninations of 1, 2, 5, 10, 25, 50, 100, and 500 francs. (No coins or notes are broken down into centimes.) A central bank in Yaoundé, Cameroon, produces the currency.

Chad adopted its flag on November 6, 1959. The flag displays three equal vertical bands of blue, yellow, and red. The blue band is on the hoist side. Chad's flag combines the design and colors of the French flag with those of neighboring African countries. (By accident, Chad's flag is nearly identical to the flag of Romania.) Blue stands for the sky, the water, and southern Chad. Yellow represents the sun, the desert, and northern Chad. Red symbolizes progress, unity, and sacrifice.

"La Tchadienne" (The Chadian) is Chad's national anthem. Chadian music teacher Louis Gidrol and a group of his students wrote the lyrics. Paul Villard composed the music. Chad adopted this anthem upon declaring independence in 1960. The entire anthem, translated into English, appears below.

The Chadian
People of Chad, arise and get busy!
You have won the fight for your land and your rights.
Your liberty will be born from your courage.
Lift up your eyes, the future is yours.

Oh, my country, may God protect you.
May your neighbors admire your children.
Joyfully and peacefully move forward as you sing,
Faithful to your ancestors who are watching you.

 For a link to a website where you can listen to the Chadian national anthem, "The Chadian," visit www.vgsbooks.com.

IDRIS ALUMA (ca. 1542–1619) Idris Aluma was the most powerful and famous ruler among all Chad's ancient empires. He ruled the Kanem-Bornu Empire from 1570 to 1603. During Aluma's reign, the thousand-year empire reached its peak of strength, size, and wealth. History remembers Aluma as a brilliant warrior and diplomat, a skilled politician, a wise and competent ruler, and a devout Muslim.

IDRISS DÉBY (b. 1952) Idriss Déby is the president of Chad. He was born in the northeastern town of Fada. He's a member of the Zaghawa people. After completing school, he trained to become a military officer in N'Djamena. Then he earned a professional pilot's license in France. He returned to Chad in 1976 and served in the army under Félix Malloum. In 1979 he switched his loyalty to Hissène Habré. Under Habré he gained a reputation as a brilliant commander. In 1990 Déby overthrew Habré. His presidential record is mixed. His government has introduced multiparty politics and built an oil industry. But it also has a high level of corruption and tends to limit freedoms.

FÉLIX ÉBOUÉ (1884–1944) Félix Éboué was a prominent and respected colonial leader of Chad. He was born in Cayenne, French Guiana, to a middle-class French-African family. He won a scholarship to attend secondary school in France and then trained for a colonial career in Paris. He served in Oubangui-Chari, Martinique, and Guadaloupe before becoming Chad's lieutenant governor in 1939. He became AEF's governor-general in 1941. He gained fame for promoting reforms and supporting Free France in World War II. He died after a heart attack in Cairo, Egypt.

HISSÈNE HABRÉ (b. 1942) Hissène Habré was the president of Chad from 1982 to 1990. He was born to Daza herders in northern Chad. After primary schooling, he worked for the French colonial government and then earned a scholarship to attend a university in Paris. He returned to Chad in 1971, worked briefly for Tombalbaye's government and then joined Chad's northern rebels. He became president in 1982 by overthrowing his former ally, Goukouni Oueddei. Habré's regime killed about forty thousand and tortured another two hundred thousand political enemies. Idriss Déby overthrew him in 1990. He fled to Senegal and lived freely for ten years. In January 2000, he was placed under house arrest there to await trial for war crimes and crimes against humanity.

MARIE-CHRISTINE KOUNDJA (b. 1957) Marie-Christine Koundja is the first published female Chadian author. She was born in the eastern town of Iriba. After secondary school, she studied law for one year at the University of N'Djamena. Then she attended secretarial school in Yaoundé, Cameroon, and worked for various Chadian agencies there before becoming the minister of foreign affairs at the embassy of Chad in Yaoundé. She published her first novel, *Al Istifakh ou l'idylle de mes amis* (Al Istifakh or the Romance of My Friends) in 2001.

KALTOUMA NADJINA (b. 1976) Kaltouma Nadjina is a Chadian sprinter. She was born in the town of Bol near Lake Chad. In the 1990s, she gained fame in Chad as one of the nation's top runners. In 1997 the International Olympic Committee arranged a grant to help Nadjina move to the United States. In 1999 she moved to Canada to train with a former Olympic coach there. She has won several gold medals and other honors in the 200 meters and 400 meters and competed in the 2000 and 2004 Olympics. She holds the Chadian women's records in the 100 meters, 200 meters, 400 meters, and 800 meters.

JAPHET N'DORAM (b. 1966) Japhet N'Doram is a famous Chadian soccer player. He was born in N'Djamena. He began his soccer career there and then joined a top African team in Cameroon. His goal-scoring skill attracted many European scouts. He played for several years on the French team in Nantes and then played one year for Monaco. He retired in 1998 after an injury. Since then he has worked for Monaco as a scout and for Nantes as sports director. His professional nickname is the Wizard.

FRANÇOIS TOMBALBAYE (1918–1975) François Tombalbaye was the first president of Chad. He was born near the southern town of Koumra to a Sara family. He was a teacher and union activist. In 1959 he became leader of the Chadian Progressive Party. When Chad gained independence in 1960, Tombalbaye became its first president. His government was tyrannical, and its policies blatantly favored southerners. These problems, combined with an incompetent civil service and high taxes, sparked a rebellion in the mid-1960s. This rebellion grew into a decades-long civil war. As Tombalbaye's regime continued, his abuses worsened until a group of fed-up military officers assassinated him in 1975.

Note: In 2008 the U.S. Department of State issued a Travel Warning to Americans stating, "American citizens should defer all travel to Chad due to the unstable security situation throughout the country. Armed rebel groups resumed activity in eastern Chad in mid-June and present real dangers. The Chadian government is unable to guarantee the safety of visitors in most parts of the country." For updates go to www.vgsbooks.com for a link.

ABÉCHÉ Abéché is the best preserved of Chad's old cities. Its long history stretches back to the 1500s. Though the city stands in the middle of a war zone and an enormous refugee crisis, many of its historic buildings and ruins survive unscathed. With its old mosques, narrow streets, open-air markets, sultan's palace, and other aging buildings, it resembles an ancient Middle Eastern city.

BOL Bol is a town on the northeastern shore of Lake Chad. Although the lake is drying up, a finger of water still reaches Bol year-round. This access—plus thriving trade with Nigeria—makes the town fairly prosperous. It's a good place to hire a boat and set off for a cruise on a vanishing natural wonder. Visitors see floating islands, herds of hollow-horned Kuri cattle, and huge flocks of birds. Sharp-eyed tourists may see hippos or freshwater manatees.

GUELTA D'ARCHEI The Guelta d'Archei is the most famous guelta in the Sahara. The Guelta d'Archei is home to several kinds of animals, including the Nile crocodile. Its crocodile population is one of the last known colonies in the Sahara. The area also has prehistoric rock paintings, slot canyons, bizarre rock formations, and huge natural arches. The Guelta d'Archei lies 50 miles (80 km) southeast of Fada in the Ennedi Desert. Visitors reach it by hiking for a few hours from the nearest place an all-terrain vehicle can approach.

N'DJAMENA Chad's capital city, with its international airport, road network, and lively economy, is the easiest part of the country to visit and explore. It's home to several lovely mosques and a cathedral. The National Museum in N'Djamena contains many historical artifacts and Chadian cultural exhibits. The city's Grande Marche is a large public market where Chadians sell carpets, pottery, leatherwork, and other crafts and artwork. Embassies and ornate colonial houses line the Avenue Charles de Gaulle.

ZAKOUMA NATIONAL PARK Zakouma National Park is Chad's first and most famous national park. It lies in southern Chad near the city of Sarh. The government of Chad created this park in 1963. It has an area of about 1,160 square miles (3,000 sq. km). Visitors can see large herds of elephants, as well as giraffes, wildebeests, monkeys, lions, and a variety of antelopes and birds.

animism: a belief system based on the idea that all beings and objects have spirits or souls

colony: a territory controlled by a foreign power

constitution: a document defining the basic principles and laws of a nation

deforestation: the loss of forests due to logging or clearing land for human uses. Deforestation leads to soil erosion; loss of wildlife habitat; and in Chad, the spread of the desert.

democracy: government by the people, through free elections

desertification: a process in which land turns into barren desert, caused by drought and overuse of drylands

gross domestic product (GDP): the total value of goods and services produced inside a country over a period of time, usually one year

infrastructure: the system of public works, such as roads, power lines, and telephone lines, of a country

massif: a compact group of mountains, especially one that is not connected to other chains or groups of mountains

millet: a grass grown as a grain in Chad. Millet is a staple of the Chadian diet.

monsoon: a seasonal rain-bearing wind

nomad: a person who moves from place to place in search of pasture and water for livestock or in search of better hunting grounds

oasis: a fertile place in the desert, where underground water comes to the surface

plantation: a large farm that produces cash crops such as cotton

protectorate: a weaker realm defended by a stronger realm, usually in return for control of the former's foreign relations

Sahel: a climatic zone in Africa. Not as dry as the desert, the Sahel makes up a large region to the south of the Sahara.

sorghum: a grass related to sugarcane, grown as a grain in Chad. Sorghum is a staple of the Chadian diet.

syncretism: the combination of different religious beliefs, such as the blending of Christianity with animism

tributary state: a realm (chiefdom, kingdom, or country) that pays taxes to another realm in exchange for military protection. A tributary state generally remains a separate realm with its own ruler and capital.

wadi: a stream that flows only during the rainy season. During the dry season, a wadi is an empty riverbed.

Glossary

Africa and the Ancient World. 2008.
http://dierklange.com (July 13, 2008).

This is the website of German historian Dierk Lange, who specializes in ancient African history. His fields of interest include the Kanem-Bornu Empire and trans-Saharan trade. His website offers full texts and summaries (in English) for dozens of his published academic articles. Many articles include helpful maps of ancient African realms.

Azevedo, Mario J. *Roots of Violence: A History of War in Chad.* **New York: Routledge, 1998.**

In this book, the author examines conflict and warfare in Chad from both historic and modern perspectives. He discusses the long history of violence in Chadian culture and how foreign interference has made it worse rather than better.

Collelo, Thomas. *Chad: A Country Study.* **Washington, DC: U.S. Government Printing Office, 1990.**

This is a comprehensive handbook on Chad that gives background on the nation's geography, climate, history, economy, society, political affairs, and culture.

Fearon, James D., and David D. Laitin. *Ethnicity, Insurgency, and Civil War: Chad.* **July 7, 2006.**
http://www.stanford.edu/group/ethnic/Random%20Narratives/ChadRN2.6.pdf (July 13, 2008).

This website, maintained by Stanford University political science professors James D. Fearon and David D. Laitin, explores the causes and characteristics of Chad's civil conflict.

Gordon, Raymond G. *Ethnologue: Languages of the World. 15th ed.* **Dallas: SIL International, 2005.**

This book is a window on Chad's diverse and numerous ethnic groups. It provides detailed descriptions of the many languages and dialects spoken in Chad, including locations, alternate names, classifications, and maps. It also directs readers to many other publications, such as dictionaries and scholarly articles, that discuss Chadian languages and cultures.

Nature. *Focus on Human Origins.* **July 12, 2002.**
http://www.nature.com/nature/ancestor (July 13, 2008).

This website, hosted by science journal *Nature*, provides a portal to a collection of academic articles on prehistoric Chad. These articles discuss the geology, climate, flora, fauna, and human history of ancient Chad.

OECD. *African Economic Outlook: Chad.* **2006.**
http://www.oecd.org/dataoecd/37/22/36735933.pdf (July 13, 2008).

This report is published by an international governmental alliance called the Organization for Economic Cooperation and Development. It describes recent economic developments in Chad, as well as the political and social context of those developments.

Population Reference Bureau. April 24, 2008.
http://www.prb.org (April 28, 2008).
The bureau offers current population figures, vital statistics, land area, and more. Special articles cover the latest environmental and health issues that concern each country.

UNICEF. *Chad*. 2008.
http://www.unicef.org/infobycountry/chad.html (July 13, 2008).
This website of the UN Children's Fund provides news updates, real-life stories, and statistics on population, health, education, and other issues affecting the lives of children in Chad.

USAID. *Considerations of Wildlife Resources and Land Use in Chad*. March 1997.
http://www.eldis.org/vfile/upload/1/document/0708/DOC4540.pdf (July 13, 2008).
This is the electronic version of a technical paper prepared by the U.S. Agency for International Development (USAID). It offers an in-depth discussion of Chad's plants, animals, major habitat types, agriculture, environmental management, and environmental threats.

The World Factbook. June 19, 2008.
https://www.cia.gov/library/publications/the-world-factbook/geos/cd.html (July 13, 2008).
This website features up-to-date information about the people, land, economy, and government of Chad. It also briefly covers transnational issues.

World Lakes Network. *Lake Chad: Experiences and Lessons Learned Brief*. February 2006.
http://www.worldlakes.org/uploads/06_Lake_Chad_27February2006.pdf (July 13, 2008).
This report, published by the World Lakes Network explores, in great detail, how and why Lake Chad is drying up. The investigation includes a close-up look at the region's geological, climatic, natural, and human history as well as a report on current habitat, biodiversity, and economic conditions. It also recommends sound policies for the future.

World Trade Organization. *Economic Environment of Chad*. 2006.
http://www.wto.org/english/tratop_e/tpr_e/tp275_e.htm (July 13, 2008).
This report, prepared by the World Trade Organization, describes all aspects of Chad's economic environment. It discusses contributions of all sectors to Chad's GDP, highlights developments in Chad's fledgling oil industry, describes the nation's foreign trade, and provides future predictions and recommendations.

Africa Megaflyover Air Dispatches
http://ngm.nationalgeographic.com/ngm/megaflyover/november/dispatch_0411.html
In 2004 biologist Mike Fay hopscotched the continent of Africa in a small airplane, guided by conservation maps, to see for himself how human activity has affected the wilderness. Readers can follow his journey through Chad by reading the dispatches and viewing the photos he logged in November 2004.

Chad: Cultural Profiles Project
http://www.cp-pc.ca/english/chad
This easy-to-read website is loaded with information, photos, and interesting trivia on Chadian culture. The University of Toronto and Immigration Canada sponsor this website to educate Canadians who mentor Chadian immigrants to Canada.

DiPiazza, Francesca. *Libya in Pictures*. Minneapolis: Twenty-First Century Books, 2006.
This entry in the Visual Geography Series® gives an overview of Chad's northern neighbor.

———. *Sudan in Pictures*. Minneapolis: Twenty-First Century Books, 2006.
Learn more about Chad's eastern neighbor in this title from the Visual Geography Series®.

Doeden, Matt. *Central African Republic in Pictures*. Minneapolis: Twenty-First Century Books, 2009.
Visit the Central African Republic through this overview from the Visual Geography Series®.

Ivory Wars: Last Stand in Zakouma
http://ngm.nationalgeographic.com/2007/03/ivory-wars/fay-text?fs=www3
.nationalgeographic.com&fs=plasma.nationalgeographic.com
Visitors to this website will read a riveting story about the guards at Zakouma National Park, who struggle valiantly to protect the elephants who live here from persistent poaching. The site also offers links to a photo gallery and videos of the wildlife and people of Zakouma.

January, Brendan. *Genocide*. Minneapolis: Twenty-First Century Books, 2007.
This book focuses on the genocides of the twentieth century, explaining what genocide is and discussing it in light of international law. The approach is thematic, examining causes, implementation, results, justice, and the survivors. It include a discussion of non-Arabs in Darfur, Sudan.

Kneib, Martha. *Chad*. New York: Benchmark Books, 2007.
In this book for young adults, the author reviews Chad's history and culture, giving a wealth of details on the various ethnic groups living within the country and their art, writing, food, recreation, holidays, and traditions.

Lake Chad Evaporation 1963 to 1997
http://svs.gsfc.nasa.gov/vis/a000000/a002000/a002064/index.html
The satellite images on this website show Lake Chad's dramatic shrinkage through the late 1900s. Visitors who enter the term *Lake Chad* in the search box on this page will find additional photos and animations of Lake Chad.

Photojournal: Chad Urban Migrant's Story
http://news.bbc.co.uk/2/shared/spl/hi/picture_gallery/06/africa_chad_urban_
migrant0s_story/html/1.stm

This photoessay by British Broadcasting Corporation (BBC) News follows the day-to-day life of a Chadian family who have given up on their village and are trying to improve their lives in N'Djamena.

Pitcher, Gemma, et al. *Africa.* 11th ed. Oakland: Lonely Planet Publications, 2007.

The Chad chapter of this large travel guide provides a helpful overview of Chad's wide array of natural and historical landmarks, as well as on contemporary Chadian culture. It also includes a summary of the country's history and politics.

Rural Poverty in Chad
http://www.ruralpovertyportal.org/english/regions/africa/tcd/

This website explains the nature and effects of poverty in Chad, with plenty of background information on the nation's geography, government, and economy to provide context. It also offers stories from real Chadians living in poverty. Finally, it describes programs currently under way to help Chadians lift themselves out of poverty.

Sullivan, Kimberly L. *Muammar al-Qaddafi's Libya.* Minneapolis: Twenty-First Century Books, 2009.

This book explores the origins, development, and reign of the Libyan dictatorship of Muammar al-Qaddafi.

Tayler, Jeffrey. *Angry Wind: Through Muslim Black Africa by Truck, Bus, Boat, and Camel.* New York: Houghton Mifflin, 2005.

In 2002 the author journeyed through the Sahel of Mali, Niger, Nigeria, and Chad. Along the way, he talked with both Muslim and Christian Africans, learning how deeply divided the two groups are. In his book, he vividly describes the bustling markets, busy cities, and run-down palaces he saw. He also recalls the generous people he met and the danger and corruption he experienced.

vgsbooks.com
http://www.vgsbooks.com

Visit vgsbooks.com, the home page of the Visual Geography Series®. You can get linked to all sorts of useful online information, including geographical, historical, demographic, cultural, and economic websites. The vgsbooks.com site is a great resource for late-breaking news and statistics.

Virtual Chad
http://www.tchad.org

This website, maintained by foreign aid workers in Chad, offers a wealth of reader-friendly information on Chadian culture. It also links visitors to a blog that provides news updates from Chad.

Woods, Michael, and Mary B. Woods. *Seven Natural Wonders of Africa.* Minneapolis: Twenty-First Century Books, 2009.

Discover seven beautiful natural wonders from across the African continent, including the Sahara, which crosses the northern one-third of Chad.

International Court of Justice, 36
Islam, 23, 24, 32, 44, 46, 47, 48–49,
    54, 57
Italy, 30

Kanem-Bornu Empire, 23–24, 26, 27,
    70
Kanem Empire, 22–23
kings (mais), 22–23, 24, 25, 26
Koundja, Marie-Christine, 70–71

lakes, 8, 11–13; Chad, 9, 11, 12–13, 72
languages, 4, 18, 22, 45, 50–51, 52;
    official, 45, 50–51
Libya, 8, 23, 25, 30, 32, 34, 35, 36
lifestyles: refugee camps, 43, 47, 65;
    rural, 41, 42, 56; urban, 18–19, 41, 42
literacy, 42, 45
literature, 50, 52, 70–71

Malloum, Félix, 33–34, 70
marriage, 47
media, 64
missionaries, Christian, 29, 33, 44, 49
mosques, 24, 55, 72
mountains, 9, 11; massifs, 11
music and dance, 49, 52–53

Nadjina, Kaltouma, 56, 71
names, 8, 22, 33
national parks, 18, 61, 72
natural resources, 17
N'Doram, Japhet, 71
newspapers, 64
Nigeria, 8, 34
nomads, 21, 45–46

oases, 16
Ouaddaï Kingdom, 22, 25–27, 28, 29
Oueddei, Goukouni, 34, 35

petroleum (oil), 7, 17, 36, 37, 59–60,
    61, 64–65
plantations, 29, 30
poverty, 7, 17, 25, 37, 41–42, 58, 61, 64
protectorates, 28
proverbs, 50

Qaddafi, Muammar al-, 32

radio, 64
railways, 30, 64
rainfall, 14, 18. *See also* drought
recipe, 55
refugees, 7, 19, 37, 38, 43, 65
religions, 48–50; animism, 24, 47,
    48, 50; Christianity, 29, 33, 44, 47,
    48, 49, 50, 57; education and, 44;
    Islam, 23, 24, 32, 44, 46, 47, 48–49,
    54, 57; syncretism, 47, 48
rivers, 11–13, 18, 19, 64, 80
roads, 19, 35, 58, 61, 63
rock art, 20, 55, 80

Sahara, 8, 9, 14, 16, 62, 72, 80;
    people of, 45–46, 53; routes
    through, 22, 25, 30
Sahel, 14, 16, 17–18, 62; people of,
    47, 53
Saleh, Mahamat, 52
sanitation, 42, 43
Sao civilization, 21–22
slavery, 19–20, 24, 25; modern, 25
solar cookers, 65
sports and recreation, 56–57, 71
stoves, solar, 65
Sudan, 8, 19, 25, 32, 38; Darfur,
    25–26, 27, 37, 38

telephones, 42, 64
television, 64
Tibesti Mountains, 9, 11
Tombalbaye, François, 32–33, 52, 70,
    71

United Kingdom (UK), 27, 30
United Nations (UN), 38; World
    Bank, 36, 59–60
United States, 35, 63

wadis, 13
wars, 7, 17, 32–33, 36, 37, 38, 41, 58;
    civil war, 18, 29, 33–34, 44, 71;
    World War II, 30–31, 70
water, 13, 17, 18, 42, 43
weather, 11, 14
women, 40, 43, 44, 47, 49, 53, 65
World Bank, 36, 59–60

Zakouma National Park, 15, 18

Captions for photos appearing on cover and chapter openers:

Cover: Two Chadian men walk by a rock formation on the Ennedi Plateau within the Sahara.

pp. 4–5 Chadians stand along the Chari-Logone River in N'Djamena, the capital of Chad.

pp. 8–9 The Sahara stretches across the northern one-third of Chad.

pp. 20–21 Ancient peoples painted these figures in caves on the Ennedi Plateau in northeastern Chad.

pp. 40–41 A group of Chadian women visit a market beside Lake Chad.

pp. 48–49 Toubou men join in a dance during a festival celebrating the presidency of Idriss Déby.

pp. 58–59 A man works in a field outside a small village in southern Chad. Most Chadians are employed in agriculture.